THEY CALL ME Pentecostal

THEY CALL Me Pentecostal

HAROLD L. BARE

Pathway

Cleveland, Tennessee 37311

Library of Congress Catalog Card Number: 92-063343

ISBN: 0871488620

Copyright © 1993 by Pathway Press

Cleveland, TN 37311

All Rights Reserved

Printed in the United States of America

Contents

Table Of Contents

Acknowledgments

Words of love and appreciation can be but paltry down payments for certain ideas.

Laila is to be largely credited with the completion of this manuscript. It was in the beginning but a mere collection of writings expressing the search for my roots.

Covenant Church has given me time for writing, and a host of friends have encouraged and assisted me with computers, finances, and technical support. I am also indebted to Professor Jeffery Hadden who has encouraged me in academic pursuits.

My parents and Laila's parents, Lonnie and Pansy Bare and Dan and Betty Baggett, have been treasures. Both of us have only wonderful stories to tell of loving parents who have modeled to us exemplary Christian living. Our heritage is rich with wonderful memories.

Finally, I am indebted to all the people who have touched my life and filled it with colorful stories. Even in adversity they have blessed me by forcing me to know and understand myself and my faith.

Introduction

A writer writes about his life experiences. The theme of this book is indeed such an intimate part of my life that it is certain my judgment and feelings dictate its course and perspective.

In fact, telling the life of a Pentecostal is a major purpose of the book. For better than half of my allotted years, I have been Pentecostal by experience. And the full 19 years of my life prior to experiencing the baptism with the Holy Ghost and speaking in "other tongues" were lived in anticipation of the phenomenon. The five years after becoming a Christian at age 14 especially were filled with praying for and desiring the experience.

It was my privilege to be born into the home of Christian parents and brought up on a full menu of Pentecostal culture. Pentecostals were not in the majority in the community. However, they were in sufficient number and of such respect as citizens that they were granted the liberty of free interaction and fellowship with each other, and the relative freedom in nonreligious matters with those not of "the fold." The fullness of this way of life has vibrated with such passion and pathos that every fiber of my being is architecturally harmonized with what I am—a Pentecostal.

Yet, if a book is to have any worth for the larger community of mankind, there must be more to a book than a simple statement of how one person feels. A Christian's debt to his fellowman is fathomless. We are our brother's keeper. It is in losing ourselves that we find ourselves. It is in loving others as we love ourselves that we come to the completeness of what we ought to be (Romans 13:10).

Therefore, that which I am dictates that I cannot write this book only for declaring my joy, explicating my knowledge, or lightening my frustrations for being misunderstood. If there is redeeming virtue for this work, it must bless the faithful, show compassion for the unbelieving, and ultimately bring glory to God.

*****

I sat on a front row and watched an hour-and-a-half service, called "The High Mass for the Resurrection," for a teenage girl who had died a tragic death in an alcohol-related car accident. She and her companion had both been drunk. Every key element of Roman Catholic dogma and government was dramatized during the Mass.

The girl was given a Christian burial, by Roman Catholic standards, predicated on her "Christian baptism as an infant." However, after the initial recognition of the death, most of the funeral dealt with matters quite outside the scope of recognizing God's sovereignty and the family's tragedy. It was a first-class selling of the Roman Catholic faith.

To my amazement, a number of the melodies sung were familiar to me. In fact, Evangelicals had composed several of the songs. In addition, there were numerous readings from books they deemed sacred, but which are not revered by Pentecostals. The Book of Wisdom was the mainstay. There were also readings from scriptures Protestants consider sacred, for example, John and 1 Corinthians.

It was during the explanation of the Lord's Supper that conception of this book occurred. The priest unabashedly invited everyone to take part in the bread and wine. However, he very specifically eliminated those who had not had a Christian baptism. He also stated that all who did take part would, by doing so, be accepting that the bread and wine were no longer that which they appeared to be, but had through priestly prayers literally become the flesh and blood of Jesus (the Catholic doctrine of transubstantiation).

What he really implied was "All of you who have not been baptized by proper procedure (via Roman Catholicism) are not welcome. But if you do come to receive Communion, you are making a statement of your acceptance of the Roman Catholic Church as the true church."

There were prayers to the Virgin Mary, for the Roman Catholic Church, and for Pope John Paul. They were all so skillfully and ritually wrapped up in the Mass that folks (many from Protestant churches) were naively affirming the words of the priest with choruses of amens.

My own abstinence from repetitions, prayers, sacrament, and so forth, gradually drew curiosity from many of those around me and from at least one of the priests. The fact is, there simply were certain parts of the Mass that were in conflict with my theology; participation would have been the sin of hypocrisy. My refusal was not a light act, but rather the acting out of my faith, which is predicated on knowledge of the Scriptures. Pentecostals simply have no right to make decisions that violate Scripture: the Holy Writ transcends human authority. To violate what is written in the Bible is to sin. I could not on the pretense of social politeness affirm doctrines which by faith are repudiated as being false and erroneous.

That day I knew this book had to be written. Hopefully, it will offer explanation to those who misunderstand Pentecostals, serve as a resource for those who academically study us, and be an encouragement to those who are and who will become Pentecostals.

It is my prayer that the reader will conclude by the evidence that Pentecostals are a biblically sound people, living honest, God-fearing lives, and walking in the power of the Holy Spirit, with other tongues being only *one* evidence of the baptism of the Holy Spirit.

CHAPTER 1

Holy Roller PK

▼ ▼ ▼ ▼ ▼ ▼ ▼ ▼ ▼ ▼ ▼ ▼

In the Beginning

Dr. Shin did not know or care that he was bringing a Pentecostal into the world. His purpose was to deliver a baby, and I was that baby. At 5 a.m. in a four-room frame house, the sounds of new life shattered the silence. Dad and my four older siblings were not in the room. Rules of our culture in those days did not allow the husband to witness the birth, and the children could very well believe that I had been delivered by midnight express from Sears and Roebuck.

Dr. Shin finished the delivery and lay a 9-pound-10-ounce boy into the loving arms of Pentecostal parents. As the new member of the family, I found my place secure, routine, and structured—eat and sleep. Getting ahead of the next arrival forced me to hastily progress beyond such dependency.

Mom was 25 when she gave birth to me. Four soon followed—adding enough children to field a softball team. Though I was the middle one, I was equally loved, nurtured, and taught the ways of the life of faith characteristic of Pentecostals. My life as a preacher's kid (PK) was to be marked by a certain discipline, remarkable for its simplicity.

The Poor—You Mean Us?

In later years I studied and taught Sociology of Poverty in a university setting. It was a great surprise to discover literature indicating that families like that of my childhood had been chronicled as being among America's poorest citizens. We had lived on a farm in Appalachia, a southeast region classically referred to during the 1960s as the nation's "pocket of poverty." It was quite a jolt for me to discover that in the world of scholars there were those who judged such poverty to be less than quality life, a thing to be pitied. Quite to the contrary, we had enjoyed our home and family, rich in love and excitement.

Being poor was not anything we consciously thought about, perhaps because we fared so much better than many other folks. For that matter, being poor was not a subject for discussion in the community. Folks did what they had to do to make it. When there were greater needs, crises, or tragedies, neighbors rallied. The hours of a day were important for providing food, shelter, and clothing. Time did not allow for the frivolities of pondering whether we were "poor" or "rich." While intellectuals may theorize and philosophize about humble living, folks who have sufficient tend toward gratitude, without polarization of "us" and "them."

If life was tough, we did not know that it was tough. It was life. We did not feel culturally deprived. What we did not have, we did not miss. If there were things in the Sears catalog that cost more than our budget allowed, the pictures could be enjoyed as we looked at the "Wish Book" for hours on end. If we did not have everything, neither did our neighbors. Folks who are busy staying alive don't have much time to worry about who is poor. While a few folks were thought of as better-off, there was neither royalty nor Rockefellers in our community. The distance between rich and poor was not great, and with everyone shopping at the same general store, social uppishness was just not kosher.

Going barefoot in the summer was a privilege, not poverty. We pleaded to our parents for permission to do so, not knowing that it was being written in the books as an indication of our "poverty." But despite our pleading, the rule was "barefoot" only from the first day of May until the last day of September, with shoes for church and school.

Benefiting from nature's blessings was a way of life. Wild berries and nuts were gathered and canned until the cellar looked like a pantry for a small army. Hundreds of quarts of jams, jellies, vegetables, and meats were carefully preserved for the winter months. Apples, pears, and potatoes were stored with care that preserved them into the planting months of spring. A meat house was filled to capacity with cured pork and other meats.

Buying groceries was more than a concern for food. Which item was purchased might well depend upon the usefulness of its container. For example, flour came in cotton bags which were colorfully imprinted. The decision of which bag to purchase was determined by who needed a dress or how that particular piece of material could be used. That same material might later be salvaged from outgrown clothes to make pajamas or underclothes. This was not poverty; it was thrift. Waste was a vice falling somewhere between sorriness and sin, deplorable in thought and detestable in deed.

Dad's Place in the Family

Dad was one of 12 children from Appalachia. Getting a high school education was a challenge, especially since there was not a high school in his home county. For fear of not getting an education, he stayed in the seventh grade three years, waiting for a high school to be built in a nearby county where he could go and complete his education. At the age of 17, he moved to Ashe County and lived with a family that required of him strenuous manual labor in exchange for room and board. During his senior year he was fortunate to live with a family of kinder disposition. Finally, at the age of 21, he graduated from high school, which at that time was the 11th grade.

Following graduation, he worked on the Scenic Parkway, then in a department store, then in a textile mill, followed by carpentry, farming, and lumber milling. Like most individuals reared rurally, Dad acquired multiple skills in the survival course of life. At the time of my birth, he was in textiles and Mom had a full-time job of mothering. With five children and another one on the way, Dad and Mom hocked their net worth to buy 33 acres of flood-ravaged farmland for $600. It was the spirit of American capitalism at its best.

His pilgrimage as a believer in Jesus was most unusual. Stirrings within his heart led him to Christ at the age of 15. He was the first of his family to experience being "born again." The simple path of religion he had chosen soon forced difficult decisions. When he gave a tenth of his income (he called it "tithe") to the church he was attending, the treasurer attempted to explain that such generous giving was not necessary. Dad felt tithing was biblical and that there must be a church that believed in tithing.

He and Mom brought their young family into the Piedmont area of North Carolina. On one occasion when he was in the forest gathering wood, Dad heard the voices of men. It was a prayer meeting of Pentecostals, members of a local Church of God.[1] Dad became acquainted with them and visited their worship services. Shortly thereafter, he received the baptism of the Holy Spirit and spoke in "other tongues."

The move to the Ashe County, North Carolina, farm in 1940 was away from a local Church of God. The family attended a Pentecostal Holiness church until Dad assumed the pastorate of a small independent church about nine miles away. In time he was able to bring the congregation into fellowship with the Church of God.

When Dad actually began to think of himself as a minister is unknown. But as Paul wrote of man's having a "calling," Dad felt he experienced it. The fact is that he had already begun to

---

[1]In this book, "Church of God" refers to the Church of God with headquarters in Cleveland, Tennessee. It is a Pentecostal denomination whose adherents believe speaking in tongues is an outward manifestation of the baptism of the Holy Spirit.

feel the calling even before my birth. God, he felt, was sending him to take the news of Jesus to others.

Entering the ministry brought tears of joy that washed away the sadness of leaving the familiar and comfortable. Long before the farm and implements were sold, our family of 10 was settled into a small five-room frame house serving as the parsonage. Dad had put farming, sawmilling, and such labors behind him to become a full-time man of the cloth. He was every inch as excited as any explorer who believes his journey is a matter of destiny.

That Dad had not attended a seminary never occurred to the family to be a deterrent. In a general way, ministers with seminary training were thought to be liberal. Yet within the community was a Presbyterian minister of good education who lived a humble, godly life and welcomed the fellowship of all Christians. With the exception of this singular seminarian, none of the other community ministers had any formal education worth mentioning. If they had, it probably would not have impressed the folks in their pews. Folks who live close to the earth do not look for a fancy gospel so much as they look for a friendly face and loving heart.

More important than education in our community was the ability of a man to preach and then live what he preached. Dad's capacity to enthusiastically preach was second only to his integrity as a man. Sinners and Christians spoke well of him, and his spoken word was good enough to take to the bank.

Though folks respected the good life of Pentecostals, it must be made clear that neighborliness and hospitality did not remove religious barriers. Folks would pitch right in to help harvest crops, raise barns, or do whatever was needed. But when it came to religion, the barriers were higher than fence posts.

Mom's people were of German stock. Grandpa Miller owned a 114-acre farm and was the first person in the whole county to own a gasoline farm tractor, though he still kept his two roan horses. The idea of Dad and Mom getting involved with Pentecostals was not at first warmly received by the Miller clan. To the thinking of some, God prefers hard work to religion. Maybe God considers work is religion.

But to Pentecostals, work is not the reason for existence; work is the means of providing for the necessities of life. Relationships with Mom's people were a little strained in the days when Dad began to spend more and more time in church work. When a decision was made to sell the farm, it was viewed as a foolish notion by more than a few neighbors and kin.

Dad's mind was made up. He understood commitment. Walking with Christ meant being a good husband, dad, and worker. It meant paying bills, telling the truth, not cursing, not drinking, and not swearing. It also included reading the Bible, praying, attending church, and being neighborly.

Dad's mark is indelible. Whether or not my siblings and I have walked in the faith given to us, we were provided a proper foundation. We had an orientation to and understanding of the Word of God which left us with the expectation that every Christian ought to be self-confessed and clean-living. Church membership, baptism, and such things are desirable but only meaningful after a personal encounter with Jesus Christ that makes Him Lord of one's life.

As of this writing Dad is still alive. Family gatherings have the tradition of his prayer which gives thanks for the blessings of the family and the food and includes a call that "each one of us make sure we are saved and prepared to meet together in heaven." He is a rock more awesome than Gibraltar.

Discipline—A Part of Love

Mom mostly managed matters directly related to the home, with evening consultation including Dad. She was somewhere between an angel and a general. When she was in the kitchen, the savory aromas were what we imagined heaven's table to be. When she was nurse, Mom could have given Florence Nightingale lessons on tenderness and compassion. When an extra hand was needed with the farm chores, she was equal to a man.

But her wrath was to be feared more than the devil, mainly because I had never seen the devil. Call it whatever you want, she called it "correction." The worst thing was that she made the victim, whoever's feet had strayed from the path, get the switches. (The *es* for plural is intentional.) If the switches were too short or too few in number, then Mom made the trip to return with the "rods of correction." Talk about the crisis of weighty decisions for an adolescent! Let the victim stand and break switches trying to decide exactly the least that will be accepted, but not one too many.

Lest this be misunderstood, ask the nine of us children and we will tell you that it was not abuse. We deserved more switchings than we received. What was actually worse than the switchings were Mom's lectures. Holding my arm with one hand and a switch with the other, Mom carried on her one-way conversation something like this:

> "Harold, I am disappointed in you. You knew better than to do what you did. We have taught you better. It hurts me to know that you would disobey. And it hurts the Lord. Don't you know that He sees you? This is a shameful thing that you have done. I hate to have to whip you, because it will hurt me more than it will hurt you, but you leave me no choice. You must know that wrong has consequences."

Forthwith the rod. Forthwith the wailing and moaning. Yet, it was a gentle balance of love and correction that always left us with a sense of security.

Evening would come and the table would be set. There was never any recognition during dinner that one had erred—no discussion of it. Others dared not belittle or cajole. There were no saints among the children, and from time to time each of us had our unfortunate encounter with Mom's or Dad's wrath. The unwritten code was plain: Don't point fingers; that is, don't talk about others who have problems.

Only one step more remained to be experienced on the road to rehabilitation—Dad's bedtime prayers. Everyone would be gathered together for Bible reading and prayer. Down on our knees we stayed until Dad was through praying out loud. Ears did not have to be strained to hear his vibrant prayer as he would pray to God for the salvation of his family. God would hear of his love for his family and his desire that all of his children would walk in fellowship with the Lord. And that Harold (or whoever had erred) would see the need of an obedient and submitted life in the fellowship of the Lord.

Doesn't Everybody Live This Way?

When I was about age 8, I had as my chore the care of the chickens. By day they were out to feed in the open field. In the evening I gathered the eggs and secured the chickens in their shed.

One evening I forgot to close the door. It was after dark when Dad reminded me of my task and sent me to finish my chore. Being afraid of the dark, I hid beside the house and mentally counted the number of steps to the henhouse and back. Then I reentered the house, pretending the chickens were secure.

The next morning 23 chickens lay on the hillside, killed by a fox. The family suffered for weeks from the loss of the eggs and the meat the chickens would have provided.

Every family member had a place to serve. By about age 5, each child was assigned a fitting chore. Younger ones might help gather clothes for wash or carry small wood. Older ones tended the fields, milked the cows, fed the animals, and chopped wood. An interdependency was necessary. It was a quasi-symbiotic environment. If one failed, it hurt everyone.

We also knew that we lived close to the earth. We studied and understood the Bible. Our home knew no foul habits, no cursing, no swearing, no abuse, no drinking, no bad books, and no television.[2] From day to day there was a routine of chores, meals together, prayer, and times of laughter and fun. Every person in the family had his place, with none being loved more than the other. Mom had a way of fixing meals to suit the taste of each member, often preparing the same vegetable in several combinations of herbs or sauces.

We knew that we had a place in God's world. We understood God to be the Creator and the source of all blessings. We understood the love of our parents to be a type of God's love for us—steady, giving, total. We knew who we were and where we were going. And we knew that we had each other's love and support in getting there.

Probably the large size of our family gave us security from outside opposition and criticism. Mom and Dad did not complain about life's deprivations or hardships. It was a privilege to be servants of God. As for the children, we had no reason to ever be alone or feel lonely. Home was filled with pizzazz, and the clock did not have enough numbers for us to get in all our chores, church, and mischief.

Life Without Church? There Is No Such Thing!

Going to church was a given. All those in the house, even guests, were expected to be in church every service. Once my soldier brother brought home a Roman Catholic friend who said he could not go to another church. Dad told him, "If our bed was good enough for you to sleep in, then our church is good enough for you to worship in." The soldier went with us to church.

---

[2]Televisions were not yet popularized. Folks of many religions viewed the advent of television with skepticism—a marvelous invention, but encouraging sin.

If visitors did come and were not able to attend the worship services, Dad and Mom would matter-of-factly explain that they were welcome to rest and make themselves at home until the family returned from church. No family member stayed home from church to entertain guests—banish the thought.

Church was more than a gathering for the righteous. It was the center of life where families came together to share their experiences. While there was a lot of singing, praying, preaching, repenting, and rejoicing, there was also a lot of courting, laughter, and fellowship before and after the services.

Church was where it happened. The larger number of Pentecostals in a community commonly came together. It was like a reunion, with the exception that innocent-to-serious romances were part of God's coloring book, especially among the young people. And since telephones and televisions were scarce, the older folks had lots of news to catch up on before and after services.

Church Membership and Being "Born Again"

Belief in God and His sovereignty was the hub of our home, and each person was expected to make his own commitment. My school friends were shocked to discover that some of my brothers and sisters were not members of the church Dad pastored. When I tried to explain to them that a person could join only when he was old enough to accept the Lord and make a public confession, they were mystified, perhaps horrified. They insisted that my Dad should be embarrassed to have children who were not official parishioners. Apparently it never occurred to them that Dad would have been traumatized to have parishioners who did not confess Jesus Christ as personal Lord and Savior.

He believed that all of us are Adam's children, conceived in iniquity and born into sin: "All have sinned, and come short of the glory of God" (Romans 3:23). Therefore, repentance was an individual matter commanded of all. He practiced what he preached—even with his family.

An Awakening to Prejudice

By the time I was age 9, we were living in a parsonage. Life revolved around the community of Dad's pastorate. But I was not yet a Christian, much less a tongues-speaker. Dad taught and preached that we had to make our own choosing of Christ to be our Savior. I hung in the balances like a kid sent with a quarter to get eggs standing in front of the candy counter. To give my heart to God would require me to stop a lot of mischief and sin—things I knew were wrong. Yet, if I did not change, I was doomed to hell. Indecision drove me to procrastination. I was neither ready to be a dedicated Christian nor a full-fledged sinner. It was fence-straddling at its best.

But I was learning. At school, my classmates put me in a circle with four boys to fight my way out. They did not like preachers' kids. In my sinner's heart, I assured myself that it was a good thing the teacher came to their rescue.

It was also quite apparent to me that religious misunderstandings are common. Dad was not asked to do school chapel. Dad was not asked to say prayers at the PTA or community meetings. And there was a lack of understanding from teachers, coaches, and schoolmates as to why we had prayer meeting on ball game nights.

The odd thing was how we perceived all this. From a social perspective, we knew we did not live in the fanciest house in town. We knew our church was not a cathedral. We knew others saw us as not being socially "in" or worthy of being invited to places and events where the socially elite circulated. But these privileges were not expected. Lack of invitations did not necessarily leave us feeling rejected.

The story of religion did not begin like a chapter in a book. Religion was a happening. It was the dominant thread in the mosaic of life. From praying for Dr. Shin to be blessed in delivering babies to attending graveside services, our sense of man's need for God was as natural as breathing. Children knelt in prayer long before they could talk. Going to church and having family Bible readings were naturally sandwiched with hoeing corn and milking cows. There was no stripping the clutch to change gears. Religion was woven into the pattern of living with chapter and verse. God is sovereign over all. To those who are children of God, nothing is mundane.

But even though religion was natural in our home, it did not take long for a child to realize that folks had different religions. "Why does Grandpa not go to church with us?" was answered by "Grandpa is a hard-shell Baptist." The conversation was closed.

> *There was the sixth grade. Miss Porter, the teacher, was middle-aged and matronly. Most of the boys were convinced that she was a battle-ax. Fair or not, we were sure that she had been a drill sergeant in WWI. If she liked boys, there was no convincing evidence.*
>
> *Her wrath seemed to gather like a storm in my direction. Mom and Dad did not allow us to dance. Miss Porter insisted that PE should teach us the social graces of dancing. If there were protective laws, I knew nothing about them; and no one came to my rescue. My sentence was to sit in the bleachers, watch the dancing, and be punished with a lower grade for not participating in an "academic" subject.*
>
> *I remember this as my first C on a report card. Needless to say, nostalgia affords me no wonderful memories of grade six. And, to this day, being friends with Porters is in spite of their name.*

The mechanics of why and how were not clear, but walls were being built up within and around me. I was coming to understand that some folks think they are better than others.

While we were beginning to understand that we were different, it was not painless. Ironically, we had our own well-intentioned prejudice. We knew that some who looked down on us lived lives of misery. We also had folks from other churches tell us they wished their pastor would preach the Bible and stop running the church like a country club. We believed we were being obedient to God in living the way we lived and loving God as we loved Him. Our comfort was in the sweet knowledge of simple and honest God-fearing living. Our hearts were saddened that those who looked down on us would not go to heaven, unless they too made God the center of their lives.

Good Dr. Shin had done his job well that March night, but he had not prescribed any medicine for my Pentecostal socialization. The years rolled along with vigor, full of experiences and challenges. If there were times of difficulty, there were far more occasions for triumph. My understanding was broadening, often being coaxed (at times not gently) by teachers and a world that seemed eternally bent on dividing people by social class and religious status. We did not yet fully understand that the compulsion to belittle accompanies prejudice. Trying to make others feel they are of lesser worth is usually founded in the critic's own insecurity. Love, the alternative to prejudice, accepts others as being whole people.

Reactions to the Prejudice

Two factors made it especially difficult for me to understand people who felt they were better than others. First, there was the very practical matter that in a family with nine children, it is impossible to have a swollen ego. If it is difficult to be honored as a prophet in one's own country, it is more difficult to have angelic wings in one's own household. Nature provides ample opportunities for personalities to clash and defects to show. Soapbox religion has little value where elbows rub together at the breakfast table.

Our perspective of life was mostly determined by our experiences. Our world was filled from getting-up time to going-to-bed time with duties and pleasures, all regulated around three-times plus per week of churchgoing. Thus, the deduction was that folks around the world faced daily duties and crises that should keep them humble in terms of their attitude of themselves and make them tolerant of the mistakes of others.

Second, the upbringing of a Pentecostal child is not left solely to the vicissitudes of life. There is practicum. The religion of Sundays pervades the weekdays, with as many comments and religious sermonettes as are necessary for the separate challenges. Scripture is quoted for everything from why folks ought to believe in Jesus and the church to why folks ought not to swear or chew tobacco. At the root of this emphasis is the straightforward belief that God made man, and therefore no man is any better than another.

The socialization of a Pentecostal child includes learning about social class, but without really comprehending prejudice. To be prejudiced is to compartmentalize life. This is contrary to the Pentecostal's value system which structures life into an integrated whole. While prejudice divides, belief in God makes all things codependent, a vital part of a beautiful, perfectly balanced completeness.

Prejudice allows an individual to do activities contrary in nature but feel no conflict. This schizophrenic approach argues for the individual to assign value on a seriatim basis. The result is manipulation of inner conflict and guilt. Pentecostals are not allowed to compartmentalize values. All of life is one package. For this reason, our parents often denied certain events that were perceived as having negative social results.

The child may understand and accept the cultural mold, but such an understanding does not assuage the pain of rejection by peers. Whatever I saw in my world, or thought I saw, by my teenage years there was a line of demarcation more real than the Mason-Dixon line: religion was not a unifying force, but a dividing one.

I had been born into a family viewing the world from a Pentecostal perspective. It was a comfortable and warm world espousing all the virtues that are worthy of man in his finest form. Knocking at our door had come various individuals to tell us that we should not be so happy, that there were "others" who did not like us, and that others believed contrary to us but were just as happy. Whether we chose it or liked it, our world was divided by outsiders into two parts: Pentecostals and others.

We accepted this division. However, we did not perceive it as being antagonistic, only a matter of reality. We were taught to love and pray for those who persecuted us. Social injustices only encouraged prayers and acts of kindness for would-be enemies.

We were taught that our first responsibility was to God and the Bible. What others did was given little value in relation to making decisions or determining our behavior. What is "right" was the forceful question, with the logical ending that every man will stand before God for his own deeds.

This sense of being responsible for our own social actions enabled us to interact without compromise or tension. Pragmatically, it is not an "us" and "others" situation, so much as it is two worlds on the same planet—the one walking in harmony with the Creator and the other in rebellion to the Creator.

While Pentecostals are for and against a lot of things, there is not an inbred negativism toward people. The pejorative nature of their faith is against activities, habits, or ways of life that are believed to be contrary to the Bible. However, Pentecostals recognize human frailty, noting that the grace of God saved, and saves, from sin. The perception is that a Christian has been saved by grace, a grace that is available to every person without prejudice or distinction.

CHAPTER 2

Looking Over the Shoulder at Things Past

▼▼▼▼▼▼▼▼▼▼▼▼

A Short History

The Pentecostal revival did not occur in a vacuum, but was a culmination of events in the 1800s. Charles Conn, a Pentecostal historian, has observed:

> Darwin's theory of evolution became one of the most divisive lines of combat. Sophistry replaced theology. The thought of Kant, Emerson, Newman, Voltaire, Schleiermacher, Carlyle, and a confusion of theologians, philosophers, and poets came to exert a greater influence on many a fashionable pulpit than did the Word of God. The Bible was largely forgotten. This hastened a deterioration of the evangelical life of the church.[1]

Albert Hyma has similarly written that modernism and socialism in churches caused a decline in attendance and general loss of interest in religion.[2] Churches had aborted their mission of exalting God. Doubt was cast even from pulpits as to whether there was a Creator God. The gospel that was preached implied that salvation was achievable via social good deeds.

---

[1] Charles W. Conn, *Like a Mighty Army* (Cleveland, Tenn.: Pathway Press, 1955), p. xx.

[2] Albert Hyma, *World History: A Christian Interpretation* (Grand Rapids, Mich.: Wm. B. Eerdmans Publishing Company, 1952), p. 355.

God was not declared dead; He simply had been sent back to His heaven, thus leaving man in charge of the world.

Individuals within many churches began to yearn for a return to the Bible. They believed faith in God was the reason for existence, not an ancillary theological or philosophical notion. Thus, the Holiness Movement was born.

Fertile soil was provided for a religious movement. Mainstream churches were stagnated. The world was in the throes of birthing an explosion of scientific progress. Steamships, trains, the telegraph, and countless other technological advances were pushing man into the future. And in the midst of all this, the Holiness Movement was paving the way for a return to God.

Many early Pentecostals were probably unaware of their historical roots in the Holiness Movement. They were looking for a personal experience with God, not an understanding of historical or current events. They wanted their faith to be real for their everyday lives. Records indicate peaceful action and an interest in uniting believers of all churches in a return to God.

What resulted was an international religious movement. After years of hoping for reform within mainstream churches, small churches were started, more in an attempt to survive than to evangelize. The infancy of the movement made it difficult to be concerned about the larger world. Threats and persecution by opponents were immediate problems. Every effort was made to simply preserve the preciousness of this newfound experience.

The marvel is that the Pentecostal Movement did not begin in one place but many. The Church of God dates tongues among its believers to 1896.[3] Assemblies of God authors Burgess and McGee indicate that Pentecostalism in America has its origins at Topeka, Kansas, in 1901.[4] In 1906 a black minister, William

---

[3]Conn, p. 25.

[4]Stanley M. Burgess and Gary B. McGee, eds., *Dictionary of Pentecostal and Charismatic Movements* (Gran5d Rapids, Mich.: Zondervan Publishing House, 1988), pp. 2-3.

Seymour, traveled to Los Angeles, where tongues became a well-publicized phenomenon of the 1906 Azusa Street Revival.

However, while Azusa Street has its significant place in history, there is no consensus of scholars as to its preeminence in the Pentecostal Movement. Pentecostalism was happening in many places in the world. For example, Minnie Abrams, a missionary of the Methodist Episcopal Church to Bombay, India, received the Holy Spirit in 1905. Willis Hoover is further cited as reading a book by Abrams which in 1907 led him to receive the Holy Spirit with tongues. He became the father of Pentecostalism in Chile.[5]

Pentecostalism began to be reported in distant lands and places without connection between the separate occurrences always being obvious. Further, scholarship must allow that with such varied documented occurrences, the probability is great that tongues happened in places of which there is no historical record.

The point here intended is that there had been a fresh outpouring of the Spirit and this outpouring was accompanied by speaking in other tongues. Etiological attempts risk demeaning the significance of modern Pentecostalism, thus giving man or an organization credit for a prophetical and divine act of God. Scholarship never force-fits data to mold to a rational schema. Until there is irrefutable evidence to the contrary, the "baptism of tongues" appears to have no common point of origin this side of the Dark Ages, that is, one person, one place, one time.

Before the Great Depression, a number of Pentecostal organizations had been established in America. Hopes for awakening the mainstream churches had declined, and the break with these churches was reasonably complete. A new era lay ahead. The Pentecostal Movement connected with the grass roots, where

---

[5]Ibid, p. 445.

people were in need, and it marketed a product offering hope in a desperate world.

Teaching and instruction were given greater significance. Publishing and education became necessary to connect the growing numbers of churches and to take revival to other communities.

God and Truth

Pentecostal thinking asserts that the will of God is the only rule by which man should live and worship. Worship is not a hobby or pastime, nor is it to be taken as a ritual, tradition, or custom. The second commandment (Exodus 20:4, 5), which objects to idols, keeps Pentecostal churches relatively free of icons. Dependence upon physical objects or ritualistic acts is perceived to range from spiritual immaturity to paganism, a violation of the commandment against idols. "God is Spirit, and those who worship Him must worship in spirit and truth" (John 4:24, *NJKV*).

Man attains his highest form when he discovers his God-given potential and the life-purpose of that potential. Truth without deviation, has reference to knowledge of the Bible, thus knowledge of God. From the time of the individual's personal acceptance of Christ, Bible reading and prayer become daily standards. Bible studies in the church and home are the warp and woof of the very culture. All the separate roles of an individual's life are packaged into one sum total which progressively ambitions to model Jesus Christ.

Style of Service

Individualism. Individualism is encouraged, even maximized. Lay ministries abound. Expression of ideas in worship are given wide latitude. Testimonies, songs, prayers, and Bible readings are a natural part of the worship, though the actual components, and their order, vary by ethnic orientation or geographic locality. Generally, the worship structure is predicated in the tradition of the Christians of the first century.

Ministers and leaders seek to include the various parts of worship as understood from New Testament history. All of these variables may or may not be included in any one service, but over the course of several meetings there is a full complement.

Singing. When the singing begins, it is a signal to worship. Pentecostals enjoy their spirited, enthusiastic, up-tempo singing, which is filled with expressions of joy and hope in Christ. The themes of salvation, victory, and heaven resound in a thousand verses offered with different notes and words.

Testimonies. Testimonies spice a Pentecostal service like beautiful flowers in a green lawn. Folks feel the liberty to share God's blessings and the miracles they have experienced in their lives. There is liberty for each person to be an active participant in the worship.

The Message. By the time for the sermon, folks have their minds off the mundane happenings of life. A little handclapping and praising the Lord has freed them from the captivity of their personal world. A sense of unity prevails—inexplicable, marvelous.

The minister's message is the capstone of worship. It is acceptable to use notes or an outline, but folks expect an extemporaneous style. Humor may be tastefully inserted. Anecdotes, stories, and illustrations help folks forget about the clock. Typically, there is a call to prayer and an invitation for sinners to become Christians.

As a Lad in These Services

In truth, many times the excitement was too much for a young lad. By the time the preacher would be inviting folks to the altar, I would be asleep. If folks began to praise the Lord with generous enthusiasm, I would be stirred from my sleep. One such awakening was most fortuitous.

I had fallen asleep on the front pew only to awaken with a start. Just inches in front of me was a thunderously large woman with her arms lifted as she praised the Lord. Frantic movement on my part got my body clear just as 300 pounds plus came down solidly where I had so recently been sleeping.

From that day forward I avoided the front pew. (It is noteworthy that I have never seen anyone, observer or participant, injured while the Lord is being praised.)

Social Sins

Social sins were hit hard by the early 20th-century leaders of the Pentecostal Movement. Drinking, cursing, dancing, gambling, and worldly entertainment were labeled as sin, often arousing violent protests from those in the community. Confrontations occurred, and the result was often unpleasant. Yet, it is fair to note, a good many of those who came to persecute these enthusiastic believers were persuaded to depart from their "sinful ways" and join the growing movement.

Terminology Associated With Pentecostals

There is no science that is omnipresent to ensure that names are scientifically related to what they identify. Labeling tends to follow the event or product, and may or may not be definitionally appropriate. The inventor's name, place of the invention, or a product used may be the basis for a name. Herewith is an attempt to present definitions of terms most closely associated with Pentecostalism.

Christians. After the ascension of Jesus, the gospel spread rapidly from Jerusalem. Persecution of believers drove them to look for homes in other countries. As they fled for their lives, the Holy Spirit empowered them to a lifestyle different from their native culture. In Antioch the believers came to be labeled with a name that sticks to this day. They were called "Christians" (Acts 11:26).

There is a paradox involved with this labeling. While much of the impact of the Acts of the Apostles is related to the Holy Spirit, the people of Antioch did not call the believers "Holy Spiriters," or "Holy Ghosters." While the term Christian may have been meant to be a despicable one, it nevertheless was intended to identify the believers as acting like Jesus Christ.

Protestantism. During the centuries that followed, various bands of Christians assumed countless subtitles. Then came Martin Luther, who broke with the Roman Catholic Church and founded the "Protest-ant" movement. Over the centuries, Protestants have divided among themselves, choosing different names and emphasizing particular doctrines, governmental systems, or social practices.

Holiness. During the early part of the 1800s, a revival movement occurred. The social gospel of mainstream Protestant churches had created a cry from the common man for a return to the Bible. This became known as the Holiness Movement. The revival began in the 1830s and moved into the 20th century, spawning countless churches and numerous denominations.

Pentecostal. Many followers of the Holiness Movement spoke in "other tongues," an experience oftentimes referred to as "the blessing" or "the second blessing." History does not portray these believers as particularly having knowledge of or seeking "tongues." In the revival at Shearer Schoolhouse, Cherokee, North Carolina, in 1896, worshipers spoke in "unknown tongues," only later to discover the scriptural passages affirming the experience.

Toward the end of the 1800s, there was a growing number of tongues-speakers. They emphasized in their teaching and preaching that the experience was the same as that received by those in the Upper Room on the Day of Pentecost. As a consequence, they were called Pentecostals, a term not necessarily meant to be complimentary.

Glossolalia. Derived from a New Testament Greek phrase, *glossolalia* literally means "to speak in tongues." Used within the biblical context, it refers to the ability one has to speak a language unknown to him. This is done through the anointing of the Holy Spirit.

Holy Rollers. The name "Holy Rollers" was used by opponents and persecutors of Pentecostals. So powerful was the stigma of this label that in 1915 the Church of God threatened legal action against any person or firm who referred to Pentecostals as Holy Rollers.[6] Usage of the term declined precipitously thereafter; however, into the 1950s the term Holy Rollers was still common. Pentecostals' improvement of their image via education, edifices, and publishing has probably eliminated more negatives and persecution than have threats of lawsuit.

Missionaries. For the most part, Pentecostals have a strong belief that these are the "latter days" before the return of Christ for His church. The theology of evangelization is a practical one which essentially says, "A whole lot must be done in a little while." Consequently, Pentecostals (who are included in the "Evangelical" camp) feel strongly that reaching the world for Christ is a mandate, not an option. Missionaries are vital to the success of evangelization.

Neo-Pentecostals. In 1959 Father Bennett, an Episcopal priest, was filled with the Holy Spirit and spoke in other tongues. His testimony rocked the liturgical church world, both creating division and revival. Thousands of Protestants from mainstream churches also testified to speaking in other tongues. Many of these tongues-speakers stayed in their native churches and were called "Neo-Pentecostals."

Charismatics. By the late '60s, Roman Catholics were also testifying of speaking in other tongues. This resulted in the Roman Catholic Church's calling high-level conferences and

---

[6]Conn, p. 130.

study groups. The conclusion was that speaking in tongues was biblical, and Roman Catholics could do so and remain in good standing as parishioners. Roman Catholics who speak in other tongues have generally been referred to as "Charismatics," though not all Charismatics are Roman Catholic.

In the last 20 years there has been an explosion of churches and groups emphasizing the Holy Spirit baptism and tongues. Gradually, the term *Neo-Pentecostals* has come to be used much less frequently in the popular press and church world.

On the other hand, the term *Charismatics* has increased in popularity, until it is at risk of not having definitional specificity. It often denotes a worship style of handclapping, contemporary music, and informal worship. It also is commonly used by tongues-speakers for identification, but in context to differentiate themselves from more traditional or classical Pentecostals. There is a conventional understanding that the Pentecostals are denominationally oriented, while some "Charismatics" feel belonging to a denomination is a spiritual liability. Many non-Catholic Charismatics have remained in their native churches, which are commonly thought by Pentecostals to be liturgical churches.

Classical Pentecostals. In an attempt to clarify the term *Pentecostal,* the older denominational Pentecostal churches were designated "Classical Pentecostals." While the term has a nice ring, it must be asserted that most of the folks who are called Classical Pentecostals are unaware of this label, could not define it, and would not respond to if called by it.

As the Pentecostal revival spread, the number of subtitles increased. But the term *Pentecostals* seemed comfortable to the broader constituency of tongues-speaking denominations. Members of any given denomination still today may simply refer to their affiliation of faith as "I'm Pentecostal." Hospital registers often carry this generic label. Formal names, such as Pentecostal Holiness, Church of God, Assemblies of God, Church of God in Christ, Foursquare, and so forth, are considered secondary.

Looking into various encyclopedias and dictionaries, one notes that most of these categories are collapsed. Those who speak in tongues are called "Pentecostals." All other titles and names are of a secondary nature.

The core theology of Pentecostals is solidly Protestant, with a strong emphasis on the Bible's being the verbally inspired Word of God. In some cases, the only distinctive that separates Pentecostals from their non-Pentecostal Protestant brethren is the doctrine of the Holy Spirit and speaking in other tongues. But tongues have often been sufficient to complicate or prevent Pentecostals from achieving optimal working relationships with non-tongues-speaking Protestants.

Do Numbers Tell the Truth?

"Hey, Harold, let's go to the movies Saturday," a group of my junior high friends called.

"Can't," I replied.

"Ah, come on, Harold. Go with us."

"His daddy won't let him," chirped another.

"Why not?" queried a third.

"Because he and his family are Pentecostals," answered some strange voice which I no longer cared to hear.

My exit was rapidly made with anger welling up inside: "How can I be a Pentecostal when I am not even saved?" echoed my thoughts a thousand times until about a year later when I became a Christian.

Pentecostals have traditionally placed strong emphasis on certain social behaviors or activities. This emphasis divides Pentecostals from many other Protestants with as much force as any topic, though it should be stated that the Charismatics tend to restrict social behavior less than Pentecostals.

"Abstain from all appearance of evil" (1 Thessalonians

5:22), Paul told a church. It is a mandate that has echoed for two millennia without diminishing in impact.

For some, abstinence from evil is construed to mean a "hermetic faith"—physical withdrawal from the world. This is not the practice of Pentecostals. Jesus prayed to the Father, "I pray not that thou shouldest take them out of the world, but that thou shouldest keep them from the evil" (John 17:15). Christians are to take whatever measures are necessary to refuse a part in evil.

As the Pentecostal Movement grew from small groups to denominations, the emphasis of separation was primarily in reference to social evils. A list of dos and don'ts evolved that appeared to restrict adherents to living at home, attending church, and dying to go to heaven. Gradually the conspicuous evils of drinking, gambling, adultery, cursing, and dancing were joined by restrictions not to divorce, wear makeup or jewelry, or swim in public places. By far, the records reflect that the history of this century's Pentecostal Movement has suffered more within the ranks because of these social restrictions than over differences of doctrine.

In the late 1950s, the Holy Spirit renewal began. By the mid-1960s it was flowing like a river through a host of churches, many of which had traditionally rejected Pentecostals. But with large numbers of laypeople and ministers testifying to the experience, denominations began to rediscover within their theology and church government room for these Charismatics to maintain their faith while staying in their native church. Charismatics tend to follow the social rules of their native churches, or so Pentecostals think. In many cases the social tolerance of Protestant churches radically exceeds the limits respected by Pentecostals.

While I was preaching to an Italian Pentecostal congregation on Long Island, New York, a Roman Catholic couple came faithfully to the services. They were members of a parish about 60 miles away, and their priest testified to having received the experience of tongues. After morning Mass, he would retire from the sanctuary and appear later in the basement fellowship hall, dressed in a conventional business suit. He would preach there in the Pentecostal tradition to Roman Catholics who had either experienced tongues or who desired the experience. The couple who related this story, however, would not attend the "Pentecostal services" in their parish, for fear of rejection by their families and Roman Catholic friends. Further, they did not share with family or friends about their trips to the Pentecostal church. The stigma of Pentecostals' being legalistic was a greater social price than they were willing to pay. They wanted the blessing "quietly," without their everyday lives being affected. And they did not want to risk ostracism from their home church.

The reluctance to be open with the tongues experience has been documented in literature.[7] The impact of social rules upon those who testify to speaking in other tongues does influence social behavior and place of church attendance.

Pentecostals view tongues as an evidence of the Holy Spirit baptism. The power of the Holy Spirit is not in the tongues; the tongues are only a manifestation of the presence of the Holy Spirit. Congruous with the receiving of the tongues is a life separated from sin and a commitment to remain apart from any and all practices that may cause loss of testimony or loss of salvation.

Yet, within the ranks of the Pentecostals, social trends and

---

[7]Edward E. Plowman, *The Jesus Movement in America* (Elgin, Ill.: David C. Cook Publishing Company, 1971), p. 118.

pressures create stress. The assumption is that those who speak in tongues are of God and thus cannot be of the devil. One cannot be both saint and sinner. But if all tongues-speakers are Christians, how then can radically divergent social lifestyles be theologically justified?

For example, suppose a tongues-speaking Charismatic also drinks alcoholic beverages. Most traditional Pentecostals consider drinking alcoholic beverages a sin. Yet, both of these people speak in tongues. For the Charismatic, this does not present a dilemma. He can still call the Pentecostal "brother." But for the Pentecostal, the imbibing Charismatic is openly sinning. It is then difficult for the Pentecostal to openly fellowship as a brother with the imbibing tongues-speaking Charismatic. The result is clearly a theological difference.

For the Pentecostal, this presents the paradoxical dilemma of what to do about a tongues-speaker who engages in a liberal lifestyle. Typically, the Pentecostal, rather than serve judgment of ostracism, simply withdraws from communal fellowship. It is to say, "I cannot do it, and I cannot approve it. But since you speak in tongues, I will leave it to God to judge."

With growing numbers of tongues-speakers, now approaching 400 million in the world, diversity is an accepted fact. Such denominations as the Assemblies of God, Church of God, and Pentecostal Holiness in recent years have reviewed social behaviors such as attending movies, public swimming, wearing jewelry, drinking alcohol, and, for women, cutting hair and wearing cosmetics. Some rules have been relaxed, while others have been reemphasized.

For the most part, Charismatics remain aloof from this fray, insisting that they are simply enjoying the benefits of their experience. They maintain that liberty in Christ allows for broad social privileges: "Unto the pure all things are pure" (Titus 1:15). Pentecostals flinch at such casualness, placing it between spiritual immaturity and ignorance. The result is that considerable social distance continues to exist between Charismatics and

Pentecostals, while both continue to speak in tongues. While there is a growing fraternity among leaders, the rank and file appear not to be ready for a brotherly fraternity.

History may conclude that Charismatics who have experienced speaking in tongues stayed in their liturgical churches in rebellion against the social laws of Pentecostals. At any rate, the evidence indicates that the exodus from nominal churches to Evangelical and Pentecostal churches seems to have slowed significantly.

Pentecostals believe that social restrictions are an integral part of possessing and preserving the faith. And while changes have been made to eliminate or reduce lists of don'ts, they remain true to their desire to be holy. An example of this is a "Resolution of Holiness" passed by the Church of God in 1988. The Resolution accompanied a revision of practical teachings.

> *"How many members do you have?"*
> *"Seventy."*
> *He smiled smugly. "We have 300."*
> *I knew my church had more in attendance than his. But, to him, he was beating me at the numbers game.*

The numbers game can be as carnal in the church as it is in the world. Politicians, businesses, and governments respond to the pressure of numbers, which helps to explain why churches bow to the pressure, counting the number on the roll instead of the lower number that sit in the pews.

In contrast to many mainline denominations, it is quite common for the number of people who attend Pentecostal churches to be significantly greater than the formal membership. The test of membership requires a strong affirmation of support of New Testament doctrines and a personal confession of faith in Christ as Lord. In addition, there is typically an emphasis on abstaining from social activities which would detract from one's Christian testimony.

Pentecostals also practice dealing with and expelling erring members, which probably discourages many from joining the membership. Other denominations, which show larger membership, may keep people on the roll who have not attended for years, have moved away, or who for other reasons would not meet the Pentecostals' standards for remaining in good standing as a member.

Ecumen-what?

Standing in the foyer of an ecumenical church office complex in New York City, I examined a display representing a variety of the world's major religions. Introducing this menagerie of gods was a plaque with this inscription:

"On your way to see the one God, what will it hurt to stop along the way and bow to Hare Krishna, Buddha, Confucius? (paraphrased).

More than 10 years have passed, and I still have not solved the mystery of how a man can believe wholly in one God and pay tribute to another as being a true god.

One God? One Path? During most of man's history there has been a proclivity to serve many gods. Even civilizations that primarily exalted one God generally were tolerant in allowing lesser gods to keep their places.

History postulates the Jews as establishing a monotheistic religion. Jehovah God categorically rejected the power of all other gods. No other gods were allowed in Israel, which was a direct insult to the gods of other nations. This did not establish a hierarchy of gods, nor enhance spiritual laissez-faire. The Jewish God posited eternal existence and mandated the destruction of all other gods of the peoples on earth. As if this were not a final blow, all other gods were demoted to the level of evil spirits or demonic beings and condemned to hell.

The God of the Bible slew thousands who returned to idol worship, and even withdrew blessings from the chosen when they failed to be devoted in worship and service. He insisted that the entire course of world events was a matter for His choosing, predetermined, and that man is not the prime mover. Man is a created being, with a free will, given the opportunity to choose whether he will serve his Creator or serve his fleshly nature, which is antagonistic to the Creator God.

All of this leaves man in the predicament of having to make a decision. If credence is given to the God of the Bible, then man must live in harmony with the morality of the Bible or be subject to the wrath of God. If man chooses to reject the God of the Bible, then he is faced with three questions of choice: (1) Is he a sinner out of fellowship with his Creator? (2) Is he denying the validity of the God of the Bible and asserting his own power to determine right from wrong? (3) Or is he perhaps even denying the divinity of God or the Bible? There is no room for vacillation.

Less than total devotion to the Creator is an aberration of the divine plan. Man by metamorphic thought processes has evolved an estranged relationship with the Creator. The result is that Jehovah God's choice creation—man—is loose in God's world, without a moral compass and tending toward self-destruction.

The 20th century has begged for brotherhood. Following the holocausts of World War I and World War II, the need for humanity to live together in peace has been a guiding influence in global economic, political, military, and religious policy-making. In conjunction with and compounding this pressure for peaceful coexistence has been an explosion of knowledge unprecedented in recorded history.

Twentieth-century academic man has sought to shed the final shackles of his commitment to institutional religion.

Commitment to religion, or any of the morals inherent in religion, is a matter of man's choice. That man has the right to make this choice is indeed a fundamental tenet of the Judeo-Christian tradition. However, 20th-century man has surged beyond his ancestors to declare that if he does not choose to make the choice in favor of Jehovah God, there will not be any negative consequences. The hell of the Bible has been postulated as being only a part of man's volition: If man wills hell, then hell exists; if man denies hell, then it is no longer a reality.

The destruction wreaked by World War I, the rapid development of technology, and secular social trends have all combined to create a climate hostile to the nature of Pentecostals. By the 1950s, man had learned to separate science from God and thus removed from God's portfolio the right to sit in judgment on social affairs. God was henceforth restricted to mystical affairs, leaving it man's prerogative to solicit divine assistance as needed, if needed, or when desired.

Now God has been neatly relegated to a respectable corner of man's world, only to be brought out for such exercises, rituals, ceremonies, and occasions as man himself shall dictate. The Creator is possessed of the created. The created defines the limits, powers, rights, and privileges of the great spirits, and of God himself, if he chooses to acknowledge there may be a God. Pentecostals view this as fulfillment of Romans 1:25: ". . . who changed the truth of God into a lie, and worshipped and served the creature more than the Creator."

In the classrooms, divinity is an abstraction. Science is god. In fairness, this may not be a matter of intentional malice. It is simply the distance that exists between scientific laws and religious laws. One is measurable and testable, and the other is mystical.

Insight into this paradox is obvious when one examines departments of religion in universities. Certainly, it is rare to find a university professor of religion who is a committed zealot to any religious cause. Professors who teach religion may even be agnostics or atheists. While scholarly books are written, no great evangelist of the 20th century has begun with his pulpit in a university classroom. And to find professors who are devotedly and conspicuously Christian is rare. It is difficult for the fire of a zealot to burn in the heart of a man who has sold himself to rationalism. The dialectical process whittles truth into human form.

Subject matter is rationalized from an academic perspective, with little regard to the personal beliefs of students or society in general. There follows the rational argument that academics cannot be rooted in faith. However, the more concretely this argument is built, the more adamantly is posited placing God, or faith in God, outside the classroom.

With several generations having been schooled in classrooms hostile to faith, it is not surprising that the general tone of today's society is one that diminishes God as sovereign. Media networks and publications do not integrate religion in the daily life of man. In recent years, published articles on religion by secular presses have been from mildly to acutely negative, emphasizing the esoteric more than the normal function and life of the individual believer in his community church. Simultaneously, the word *luck* has increased in conventional usage to explain phenomena that once were attributed to deity.

Devaluation of God has increased the number of gods seeking viability in the marketplace. The social climate of the world is one that serves as an incubator for developing new religions and new gods that can offer man his hopeful utopia. The weird and the unusual are encouraged, tolerated, and marketed. For example, daily news coverage gives nothing of the normal life of religious adherents. "News" of religions is conspicuously bizarre, criminal, and deviant.

The inevitable consequence is a proliferation of gods and goddesses and cults. In the 1950s, Daddy Grace and Father Divine insisted that they were "God." Today the number of those who claim to be divine is in the tens of thousands. While this is not an altogether new phenomenon, it must be stated that the God of the Bible has never before been so frequently asked to give equal time to Hare Krishna, Sun Myung Moon, Buddha, and various swamis or gurus. Strangest of all is that this move of ecumenism of religions includes leaders from the Christian community.

Many rich, famous, and powerful individuals openly oppose the very tenets that are predicated in the Judeo-Christian belief of God. The World Council of Churches allows for reverence and homage to be paid to various deities, a diversity of faith with the brotherhood of mankind. Mormons insist on Jesus Christ's being a god, but also insist that each of us can be equal to Jesus.

The circus becomes wilder and the merry-go-round gets faster. The message is that folks who still insist that religion, as per the Bible, is the essence of life are perceived to be behind the times, out of sync, out of kilter, and perhaps even lacking in intelligence.

Pentecostals often get pitched in with whoever or whatever is not liked about religion. It is not certain why, but some of the worst stories that can be told about religious zealots are told of Pentecostals.

Why All the Fuss? The predication of a "born-again" experience clearly separates Pentecostals (and other Evangelicals) in ideology from many of the world's "great" religions. Man cannot do righteously without Jesus Christ. With Jesus Christ, man ought not to do wrong. If he does, it is sin. The grace of God embodies victory and disclaims wanton living. Life in Christ is a venture begun at the Cross by pleading for the blood of Jesus to cleanse from all sin. Joyously, "whosoever shall call on the name of the Lord shall be saved" (Acts 2:21).

What results is a standoff that is unmitigated. If the Pentecostal gives equal credence to contradictory religions or faiths, it opens Pandora's box: All other gods, the belief in no god, or the belief that man is god must be accepted on a par with the deity of Jesus Christ. Pentecostals would be forced to accept the diversity and equality of gods and man's right to create social laws contrary to the Bible. Such conclusions are anarchic and would be diametrically opposed to Pentecostal roots.

Pentecostals remain monotheistic, with all conviction that the God of the Bible is the only God. And they believe that God still expects and desires nothing less than total commitment from each individual. There is no room for halfhearted commitment. There is no room for other gods. There is no room for man to be his own god. There is room only for faith in and service to the God of the Bible.

Proponents of false gods expect commitment. Millions worship Buddha, Hare Krishna, Mormonism, New Age ideas, and so forth. They hold their way to be truth. They make no apologies for their insistence that their way is the right way.

And Pentecostals make no apologies for believing that Jesus Christ is the only Savior for all mankind. Welcome to the real world of the Pentecostal.

CHAPTER 3

Basic Tenets
of Pentecostalism

▼ ▼ ▼ ▼ ▼ ▼ ▼ ▼ ▼ ▼ ▼ ▼

Newspapers, magazines, radios, televisions, and telephones confront us with new knowledge, happenings, controversies, variations, and conflicts. The idea is that we are all on the same planet and therefore share life in common. The truth is that we struggle for individuality and resist being folded into statistical tables. Our lives are so researched and standardized that we are told how many calories we ought to consume, what books we should read, and what stylish colors we should wear.

Against such a backdrop, it is extremely difficult to work out a religious belief that has peculiarities and specificities that differentiate it from other religions. Few insults are more divisive than to say that one has a possession, especially a religious belief, that is more precious than that possessed by others.

The thrust of 20th-century social thinking has been to suggest that human behavior is relative. Several decades of secular social thinking have evolved into humanistic thought that much of what man does is neither right nor wrong, good nor bad. Logically, the consequence of this reasoning is brutal rejection of any person or group of people who claim, in the name of any god, that man is not the master of his own destiny.

But given that a religion is to be functional for its adherents, it must have distinctives or cease to exist. Survival of a set of religious beliefs requires an orderly system of essentials. The number and type vary and may or may not make sense to those outside. But for those within, acceptance of these basic beliefs is a rite of passage.

Following are 10 basic tenets of the Pentecostal faith. These beliefs, shared by major Pentecostal denominations, are not listed in any particular order. All are essential to the faith.

The Bible Is Inerrant

Pentecostals believe in the verbal inspiration of the Bible. Simply put, this means the whole Bible is inspired of God and is to be believed.

"Theological hairsplitting" is ecclesiastical jargon. The implication is that much ado is being made over a rather trivial matter.

Inerrancy of the Bible has often been targeted as a semantic difference with too much fuss for the subject matter. Those who believe the Bible does have translation, dating, and doctrinal errors tend to insist that their position is the only intelligent and scholarly position. To the contrary, those who accept the Bible as being verbally inspired tend to view their critics as being somewhere between hypocrites and heretics.

The result is not "hairsplitting" but chasms of distance that separate the two camps. More than a cold war, the fragmentation often leads to charges that the other side has defected from the faith to become a diabolical tool of Satan or that practicality and testimony have been forfeited in the interest of petty doctrinal positions.

Interesting paradoxes are involved. When Pentecostals are labeled as "inerrants," it may be intended to hurt, yet it may be received as a compliment. "Why should the truth be argued?" they would respond. "Life is too precious and our task is too great to waste time debating issues that are already settled."

For the most part, in the Pentecostal classroom, pulpit, and pew, acceptance of the Bible as being doctrinally without error is a given. Scholars within the ranks may be able to cite dates or words that are debatable in terms of accurate translation. However, carrying such knowledge to the rank and file, advocating it in a public way via preaching or teaching, or authoring it with a negative position, would be anathema. No Pentecostal individual or ministry could withstand the loss of integrity that would straightforwardly be the consequence of opposing inerrancy.

Esprit de corps is often built via attacks against those who have departed from the faith to rewrite the Bible or cast aspersions on its accuracy. A sense of unity and loyalty intensifies the need to stand unequivocally as advocates of the Bible's being God's Holy Word. Those who reject this position are cast as enemies of the truth and perpetrators who would change the truth into a lie.

Tolerance for those who offer that the Bible may be errant is perceived as liberalism. And there is precious little room for such tolerance. There is likewise little tolerance between the different camps. Those who believe the Bible is errant often attempt to portray the literalists as being less than scholarly, with inclinations toward fanaticism, and infected with a disease of appealing to emotions rather than reason. To all of these invectives, those who hold to inerrancy simply respond with a loud cry: "Liberals."

For certain, if there is any hope for fraternalism, those who would attempt to draw Pentecostals into discussion would do well to leave alone the argument of inerrancy. Believing that the Bible is true—every word of it—is as integral to faith as the heartbeat is to life.

New Birth Through Jesus Christ: The Only Way to Heaven

Jesus said: "I am the way, the truth, and the life: no man cometh unto the Father, but by me" (John 14:6). Pentecostals believe the only way one can enter heaven is by believing on the Lord Jesus Christ, repenting, and accepting forgiveness through Him for sins.

Pentecostals view life on earth as the pursuit of the city of

God, a consuming pilgrimage terminated only by death or the coming of Christ. Faith keeps hope alive. Faith in things to come enables rejection of mortal temptations. No earthly pleasure is to be preferred to the commitment of walking the path to the Holy City.

To frustrate the simplicity of this faith, there is the growing challenge that various cultures honor gods not associated with the God of the Bible. While the existence of many gods is not new, modern technology has afforded means of travel making the world a community and not just a conglomeration of isolated, individual civilizations. New disciplines such as psychology, sociology, and anthropology, all predicated in man's scientific laws, serve to argue the right of man to live in peace with gods of his choosing and laws of his making, or so the myth is propagated. As man's world becomes smaller, he views life on planet Earth as being far more important than the mysticism of life beyond biological death.

While man is geographically brought together by modern transportation and electronics, an abysmal chasm has developed which, to Pentecostals, denies coexistence of the differing gods. As decades and events have unfolded, distance between Pentecostals and those who would by human effort make earth a paradise has increased to immeasurable proportions. And those gods which give man power to right the world are but idols to the Pentecostal. Man holds no power to right wrong or redeem the earth, except by the enabling of the Holy Spirit of God.

Pentecostals view man as part of God's creation, the Judeo-Christian God, that is. As man chooses to return to the fellowship of God, God imparts wisdom and knowledge to man to administer individual and community affairs. It is all done via the grace and power of God and to the glory of God. Those who accept and believe are perceived to have returned in wholeness of spirit and body to the fellowship of their Creator.

The irony is that most of the world's great religions consider Jesus Christ to be a holy prophet, a divine being, or a god.

However, Jesus Christ rejected every other religion as fake—"the blind leading the blind" (see Luke 6:39; John 14:6). And the Pentecostal believes that all religious leaders who deny Jesus Christ as the only Savior of man are but imitations—fakes and charlatans.

True to man's nature, if the argument cannot be won by reason and logic, the opponent must be flawed. The alternative is to strip the opponent of the right to argue by insisting that his mental faculties are deranged, deformed, or genetically impaired.

While ecumenism may sound palatable to some, for the Pentecostal, ecumenism is divisive if the terms of brotherhood require honoring any god other than the God of the Bible. Jesus is not one of the gods, not an elite among the elite, not even the Elite among other elites. He is God incarnate—the only Savior.

There is no bridge that can cross these divided waters. Epithets and invectives litter the battlefield, and the war seems eternal. Unfortunately, the distance across the abyss will only become broader, darker, and uglier, because truth, as Pentecostals perceive it, is uncompromising.

For this devotion to truth, the Pentecostal is at risk of being criticized for being "too heavenly-minded." It is a charge that has no defense. The Pentecostal sees life as having a different orientation, purpose, and eventual destiny than do followers of many of the world's great religions. And even in the present life, the Pentecostal has the intrinsic reward of a Christlike life. The greater the rewards, the less value is given to criticism. There are no superiors to love, joy, and peace.

A Sanctified, Holy Life

Salvation is free and grace is given to all. However, Pentecostals believe that after receiving salvation through Jesus Christ, one must live a holy life in order to stay in fellowship with Him. "Without holiness no one will see the Lord" (Hebrews 12:14, *NIV*) is taken to literally mean that one must continue to live a life separated from the world in order to enter heaven.

The sign read, "The Living Waters Church of Jesus Christ Sanctified Holy." Even to a dyed-in-the-wool Pentecostal, that brought a smile.

But as the miles passed, I pondered the importance of every word in the name. Especially the last two words, "Sanctified Holy," brought to mind a plethora of familiar memories.

The genetics of the 1800s Holiness Movement carried characteristics of a conservative social lifestyle. Pentecostals, the children of the Holiness Movement, inherited this strong consciousness of needing to interrelate daily activities with religious dogma.

"Be ye holy; for I am holy" (1 Peter 1:16) has been, and is, a motto of Pentecostals as familiar as Grandmother's picture album. While there is no law specifying the exact manner in which this scripture is to be applied, there is the resounding ring that the evidence of lifestyle ought to unambiguously testify of Christian distinctives.

"Sanctified" generally connotes a separation from activities that are either considered evil or that hurt one's public testimony of being a follower of Christ. Drinking, smoking, dancing, cursing, gambling, and similar sins have been commonly flagellated by holiness preachers in the tradition of Wesley, Asbury, and Finney. Such social evils are both conspicuous and generally unkind in disposition to the wholesome interest of churches.

But mere abstinence from social evils does not itself constitute the essence of a holy life. Rather, the perspective is that certain things just do not mix—the chemistry will not work. Priorities of a committed life to Christ require budgeting time, money, and thoughts in directions antithetical to a wanton life of pleasure.

Construction of a lifestyle including Bible study, community worship, Christian fellowship, and related activities molds a pattern contrasted to one's life before meeting Christ. The objective is to develop a mind-set to attain the characteristics of Christ which marked His gentleness, compassion, charity, and purity. This is the aspired life of holiness.

Pentecostals have been often roundly criticized for their reclusive social tendencies. However, from the mind-set of the Pentecostal, many of the nominal churches have been co-opted into the sociopolitical structure of society, thus negating the power of their preaching.

Such an abstract proposition as "sanctified holy" can never be converted into a formula. However, to the Pentecostal this is just as it should be. The final measure of a Christian and a local church is in its ability to be "in the world, but not of the world" (see John 17:14-16). Reduction to a simplistic formula would erase the need for personal agonizing, soul-searching prayer to discover the holy life.

It is doubtful if Pentecostals would survive if they lost this sense of urgency to be holy. If they did survive, it would be only a matter of time until they would simply become another of the nominal churches to dot the landscape of Main Street and clutter the ecclesiastical gutters with another version of religion without distinction or movement.

It would therefore appear that, for the Pentecostal, living a social life of separation will continue to be a prerequisite for obtaining the higher life of holiness. Failure of such practice and belief would be a blockage of a main artery and require major bypass surgery.

Speaking in Tongues

Pentecostals believe that speaking tongues is an outward manifestation of having been filled with the Holy Spirit.

Adam as a newly created being had been given wisdom and authority to rule the earth and its creatures. His linguistic abilities were of such magnitude that he named the animals of the earth. The Bible recounts his ability to walk and talk with God in the Garden of Eden. After Adam's sin, God withdrew this privilege until man could be taught the holiness of his Creator.

In an effort to restore relationships with God, man conceived various techniques, all of human will and human effort. The most ludicrous attempt on record to reach heaven without God was to build a tower (Babel) that would be high enough for man to physically climb into paradise.

This incurred God's wrath, and He divided into parts the single language of the earth. This prevented communication and in turn caused social division. Work on the tower ceased for lack of a common language.

Following the division of Babel (Genesis 11:9), Adam's language was lost. Tribes and nations contrived to engineer their own means of communication, building on the fragments of that portion of the language of Adam that was given them at Babel. Those who understood each other formed tribal units and geographically separated themselves from those they did not understand.

The Need for a Heavenly Language. The Bible teaches of heaven and that men will go there. It is logical that heaven's language will not be any one of the more than 5,000 dialects known to 20th-century man. Man's languages are limited, filled with negativism and profanities, and painfully void of words that would be fitting in any paradise—often such words seem not to be fitting even for planet Earth.

Further, to select an earthly language for heavenly use would be to imply that one language is better than another. While God has the right to make this choice, why should He adopt a language for an eternal heaven from a finite and temporal part of His creation? Language is evolved and contrived, filled with imperfections. To believe that God would choose man's language for Paradise is irrational.

Heaven existed prior to man. The Bible speaks of beings in heaven. Should the future language of heaven be man's language, then all the beings of heaven would have to forfeit their native tongue to speak in an earthly language.

It follows that heaven must have a language that is not culturally ascribed to any ethnic group. Whether it is Adam's language prior to the fall of Babel is a matter for speculation. What is certain is that the language of heaven will be appropriate for giving praise and glory to the Creator.

God Allows Mortals to Speak the Heavenly Language. Given that heaven has a language, it seems further reasonable that God is able to impart this language to those who abide in His fellowship. Such rationale is not an attempt to question the Holy Scriptures, but to understand. Reasoning is an ability the sovereign God has provided man, with the expectation that it will be used for God's glory.

The purposes of allowing mortal man to speak in a heavenly tongue are manifold:

1. *To exalt Jesus Christ.* The Holy Spirit's task is to care for the church that Christ founded.

2. *To build up the individual.* The individual believer is strengthened in his fellowship of prayer and communion with Christ via the prayer language of the Holy Spirit.

3. *To build up the church.* The local church is witness of the power and presence of God as the Holy Spirit enables individual believers to speak in a language not culturally or educationally acquired by the speaker.

4. *To glorify God.* The language of the Holy Spirit is expressly to glorify and exalt Christ, which is the business of man and the work of the Holy Spirit.

5. As a sign of God's presence to unbelievers. Believers and unbelievers are made to know that God has divinely intervened in the affairs of man (1 Corinthians 14:22).

The Two Types of Tongues. Pentecostals believe the Holy Spirit enables tongues both to witness in a foreign language and to speak in a heavenly language. Both are divine works and intended to exalt Christ. While both are for the joy of the believer, neither are for the glory of the believer. The express work of the Holy Spirit is to testify, or give witness, of Christ.

In Acts 2 is the version of "tongues" that is almost universally accepted by Christians. Jesus told His immediate followers to go and tarry in Jerusalem until He sent the Holy Spirit. This happened about 10 days later in the Upper Room. A heavenly language was the manifest symbol of the arrival of the Holy Spirit. Joyous worship exploded into the streets, first drawing accusations of drunkenness, but then setting a stage for Peter to preach. About 3,000 were won to Christ that day. Jews who had received the Spirit and spoke with tongues flowed through the gathering, speaking whatever language was native to the listener.

Many years after the Day of Pentecost, Paul talked with Christians in Ephesus, who told him they were born again by the power of God but insisted they had not even heard of the Holy Spirit. Paul explained to them the baptism of the Holy Spirit, laid hands on them, prayed for them, and they spoke with tongues (Acts 19:1-6).

In the case of these disciples of Ephesus, there is no indication of the presence of unbelievers or persons who spoke any language other than the native tongue of the Ephesians. Thus, there was no need for the Holy Spirit to enable the Ephesian disciples to speak an earthly language other than their native tongue. The assumption then is that they spoke in a language unknown to any man. The apostle Peter, a Jew, had had a similar experience with Gentiles (see Acts 10).

Tongues Are Needed for Today. Pentecostals believe a person may receive the God-given ability to speak in a known language other than his native tongue, as happened on the Day of Pentecost. For example, a person who does not know a word of

/

Chinese may be divinely empowered by the Holy
fluent Chinese. This would happen to serve as
invite a Chinese person to accept Christ. The s_
even be aware that the language he has spoken is Chinese.
Therefore, the intervention of God through the power of the
Holy Spirit is emphatically demonstrated.

Many of the critics of Pentecostals insist that speaking in
tongues was only for the New Testament era ministry immediately after Jesus' ascension back to heaven. The "other tongues"
they insist was a God-given ability to speak foreign languages to
speed the spread of the gospel. They conclude that once the
early church was established, and the original apostles died, the
gift of tongues is no longer necessary.

What has happened with the account of the New Testament
Day of Pentecost is part of the story of why there are so many
different churches. A simple and wonderful doctrinal treasure
gets turned into dogmatism. The Bible does not limit the number of those in the Upper Room to the 12 disciples. Luke wrote,
in Acts 1:15, "The number of the names together were about an
hundred and twenty." The popular argument that almost singu-
larly divides Christians on the issue of "other tongues" is that
the tongues were a temporary tool of evangelism to help get the
fledgling church established.

Those who look askance at Pentecostals assert that because
of the ignorance of New Testament times and the lack of linguistic skills, God enabled the disciples to speak in tongues—other
languages. This was a master plan of heaven to broaden the
base of the church by disseminating the gospel to many nations.
This argument firmly restricts tongues to the New Testament
generally, and specifically to the lives and times of the disciples.

There is a fatal flaw to this theory. The proposition is that
upon the advent of the Holy Spirit, tongues were given solely for
the purpose of witnessing. If tongues were successful enough to
make the early Christian believers those who "turned the world
upside down" (Acts 17:6), why did the Holy Spirit stop using

such a successful tool for evangelism? World population figures in New Testament times were about 300 million. Today the world's population is over 5 billion. The known number of languages and dialects in the world exceeds 5,000. More than half of these languages or dialects do not have a single Bible verse written in their native tongue.

If the larger part of the world is without knowledge of the Bible, it would make sense for the Holy Spirit to continue use of the evangelistic tool that worked so excellently in early New Testament times. Pentecostals believe that tongues, a necessary and valuable tool for ministry, was given as a part of the New Testament church. The ministry of tongues is currently an effective tool in God's divine plan for ministry to the church and witnessing to non-Christians.

Paul, who was not one of the 12 disciples, admittedly spoke in tongues. He also is reputed to have spoken seven of the cultural languages of his day. Yet, he found tongues to be an effective part of his ministry. Ironically, many who criticize Pentecostals based on 1 Corinthians 13:8, that is, "tongues . . . shall cease," fail to read in 1 Corinthians 14:18 that Paul says, "I thank my God, I speak with tongues more than ye all."

A Theological Dilemma. Those Christian denominations that do not affirm the doctrine of tongues face a theological dilemma. How do they justify calling Pentecostals "Christians" and yet speak of the doctrine of tongues as unacceptable or nonbiblical? The doctrine cannot be good and evil at the same time. How can tongues in the New Testament be a gift from heaven but now be an evil from hell?

There is no happy resolution of this problem for those who stand in opposition or with coolness to Pentecostals. Meanwhile, the number of tongues-speaking Christians continues to grow toward 400 million, and the weight of these numbers begs a new theological understanding from mainstream theologians.

Signs Following Believers: The Gifts and Fruit of the Spirit

After His resurrection, Jesus promised His followers that upon His return to heaven He would ask the Father to send to them the Holy Spirit, the "Comforter." The idea of "comfort" was that Christians would not be alone and unarmed against a hostile world. The Holy Spirit would further equip and empower the believer. Two aspects of this empowerment are the gifts and the fruit.

The gifts of the Spirit are listed in 1 Corinthians 12. Gifts of the Spirit are neither entities to themselves nor a treasure for private pleasure. Gifts are tools the Holy Spirit gives to the believer for ministry in Christ's church.

As an army trains soldiers for different tasks, so the Holy Spirit puts every Christian through "boot camp." Its focus is militant in the sense of loyalty and commitment, yet the emphasis is on service with love. Each individual is trained and equipped for specialized work/service in God's army. With the gift is also given the divine power to accomplish the assignment.

Gifts, in the larger application, are the Spirit-filled believer's ministry to others and to the church, both for the glory of Christ. Thus, signs following believers is a natural consequence of the believer's receiving these gifts (Mark 16:15-18).

Fruit of the Spirit (Galatians 5:22, 23) are results of the Holy Spirit's working in and through the individual. They are marks of maturity that one is walking in the Spirit with Christ. Individuals rejoice in their growing ability to be in the world but not of the world. They have indeed found that the most fruitful path to happy living on earth is to know Jesus Christ as personal Lord and to be filled with the Holy Spirit.

The challenge is to become a mature and useful servant. It is ceasing to consider self as priority. It is putting Christ first and fellowman equal with self. It is an aspiring life—demanding and rigorous—but with earthly rewards of ethereal value.

Ordinances: Water Baptism and Communion

All major Pentecostal denominations share the ordinances of Water Baptism and Communion.

Water Baptism. Pentecostals believe that baptism by immersion in water is to follow the experience of salvation. Water baptism is a symbolic illustration of faith in God. The second commandment rejects man-made symbols that are idolatrous in form or character. The God of the Bible is "Spirit, and those who worship Him must worship in spirit and truth" (John 4:24, *NKJV*). To be baptized in water is a literal acting out of commitment to Christ. It is a public affirmation of a private decision.

In the Old Testament tabernacle, every sacrifice was washed prior to its being presented as an offering to the Lord. While it had already been examined for acceptance, ceremonial washing in the brazen laver was a formal part of the cleansing before a sacrifice was placed on the coals of fire. Those who come to Christ and are cleansed by His blood are examined by the Holy Spirit and justified before the heavenly Father.

Water baptism is an important statement to Christians and to unbelievers that a public testimony is being made about the changing of masters. Satan is dethroned; Jesus is Lord.

Water baptism does not cleanse sin, but it is symbolic of
1. Jesus Christ's death, burial, and resurrection
2. Our own death to sin and renewal to life through Christ
3. Our own future physical death and resurrection to eternal life with Jesus Christ.

It is a sacrament of obedience, with assurance of divine blessing.

Communion. Pentecostals believe that Christians should participate in Communion, sometimes called the Lord's Supper.

Sacraments, though they may vary in form and nature, are symbolic of the highest level of commitment to one's faith. The essence of cardinal doctrines is embodied in rituals that reify faith. The Passover meal of the Jews was celebrated by Jesus and came to be known as the Last Supper. It is precisely this scene that Leonardo da Vinci depicted in his painting by this name.

During the meal with His disciples, Jesus instructed them that what was being done in the Upper Room was to be repeated by them and their converts. Because of the intimate setting of believers who repeat this custom, in time it also came to be known as Holy Communion, or Communion. Thus, the emphasis was on the community of believers sharing commonly in the remembrance of Christ's death, resurrection, and hope of His return.

The Roman Catholics, while a part of Christendom, have more definitively associated the custom of the Last Supper with the Passover meal eaten in Egypt before the Exodus. Supposedly, the bread and wine, called the "Eucharist"[1] by Catholics, are by the prayers of the priests transubstantiated into the literal blood and body of Jesus Christ.

But to the Pentecostals, the Last Supper, or Communion, is a sacrament of remembrance and renewal. The bread and fruit of the vine are but symbolic. They experience no chemical change through prayer. The holiness of Communion is in the righteousness of Christ and the pureness of the believer's heart, not in the prayers of the minister or the dogma of a religious organization.

Communion is not usually practiced weekly by Pentecostals. It may not be regularly scheduled and may be practiced only a few times each year. Whether or not each occasion is announced in advance is at the discretion of the local leaders. This is sometimes a frustration to those who come to Pentecostal churches from churches that take Communion weekly. The

---

[1]The term *Eucharist* for Communion is commonly used by those in the Roman Catholic tradition but is not commonly used among Pentecostals.

decrease in frequency of Communion is perceived as de-emphasizing this sacrament.

Theologically, there is a distinction. Communion is practiced by many churches as a progressive and necessary ritual, encompassing cleansing and salvation. To the Pentecostal, Communion is not a salvific act. It is an affirmation of salvation.

The truth is that Pentecostals are remiss in not having Communion more frequently. However, their fear of making idols of rituals—of "having a form of godliness, but denying the power thereof" (2 Timothy 3:5)—discourages marking the calendar for holy days and holy deeds. Rigidity of religion is perceived to restrict the divine right of the Holy Spirit to direct daily lives and public worship.

Communion as practiced in Pentecostal churches is usually open to all believers. While church membership may be tested for other reasons, there is the express belief that individuals have the right to answer for themselves whether they have committed their life to Christ. Such openness leaves the responsibility for participation in Communion to the individual.

Finally, it should be noted that speaking in other tongues and giving interpretations often occurs during this sacrament. Those who would aspire to an understanding of Pentecostals must never forget the importance of this parallel, if they are to give scholarly adjudication to the role of Pentecostals in society and in the church.

Divine Healing

Pentecostals believe that divine healing is provided for all in the Atonement. However, while some Pentecostals insist that God has promised to heal a true believer every time he is sick (if he asks correctly), others believe that God has a perfect will which may not include healing every time it is requested.

The Holiness Movement's emphasis on a return to the Bible

was followed closely by its insistence of the validity of the doctrines of healing and the coming of the Lord. Study of the Scriptures led those in the Holiness Movement to accept, teach, and preach these doctrines as being theologically and eschatologically sound.

For centuries before Christ, Jews taught that the Messiah would perform miraculous healings. Opening the eyes of the blind would be the *coup de maitre* of the divinity of the Messiah, as would be the raising of the dead.

Jesus' opening of the eyes of blind Bartimaeus fulfilled this prophecy. Healings of withered limbs, diseased bodies, and insane minds were all done in a dramatic prelude to raising Lazarus from the dead. He who could open blind eyes would be recognized as the Messiah.

Healing had been a mark of the prophets of the Old Testament. Abraham was enabled to father a child when he was "as good as dead" (Hebrews 11:12). Abraham prayed to God for Abimelech, and he was healed (Genesis 20:17). Moses experienced the healing of leprosy on his hand (Exodus 4:7). Jeremiah prayed for healing from God, realizing that with God's touch he would be made whole (Jeremiah 17:14). Elisha told Naaman how to obey God and be healed of leprosy (2 Kings 5:14). Isaiah prophetically declared that "by His stripes we are healed" (Isaiah 53:5, *NIV*).

For someone to perform miracles of healing was not new, even to those of non-Jewish tradition. Recorded history offers countless stories and documented cases of miraculous healings even among peoples who deny or are ignorant of the God of the Bible. Many non-Christian religions and belief systems teach and practice healings.

What was different was that Jesus healed people on a common basis, with no hocus-pocus, and with only a spoken word. Multitudes came to Him, and He healed them (Matthew 12:15). His miracles were unlimited in number and scope. He offered no potions, sold no formulas, spoke no magic words, and called upon no idol deities. He simply said, "Behold, thou art made whole: sin no more" (John 5:14). There was no strain, no secrecy, no class distinction, no hiding it in the night as a ceremony just for the elite believers.

Added to all this, Jesus directly and formally gave His disciples the authority to go out and perform the same works. On one occasion, when they complained about not being able to cast out a demon spirit, He reminded them that the power was not their own. "This kind does not go out except by prayer and fasting," He said (Matthew 17:21, *NKJV*). This charge Jesus gave to the disciples lest they should forget that the power to heal comes from God; therefore, all the glory belongs to God. In final instructions to these same disciples before He went back to heaven, Jesus gave power to them and every believer to use His name for healing. "Greater works than these shall he do" (John 14:12), He said of His own miraculous works. Mark's Gospel records Jesus' last words before His ascension: "They shall lay hands on the sick, and they shall recover" (Mark 16:18).

Perspective. Sickness and disease are great antagonists of man. Death waits as the final enemy. When man is in pain, he seeks relief. A sizable portion of the United States' annual governmental budget is spent in areas related to man's health and well-being. The sophistication of our medical system is proof that no price is too high to pay for the privilege of living—hopefully, without pain. Billions of dollars' worth of pain relievers and mind drugs are sold each year.

Rich and poor alike grope for meaning in life after death. While for some it is an obsession, for all it is a question. Reincarnation, a teaching rooted in Eastern religions, is an answer believed by hundreds of millions. They will come back to try life again, they say, though they cannot be certain whether their return will be as an animal, bird, or human. Meanwhile, they tend to face life with a stoicism, accepting pain, or with a mysticism, denying it.

People who are doubtful of life after death have their bodies cremated—a statement, they insist, of finality. However, their insistence does not remove the question of whether they have at some time doubted about the hereafter. And while they live, they must resolve the issue of human suffering and healing.

Medicine men, witch doctors, medical doctors, and religious healers share a common burden: to relieve pain and suffering. By whatever means this goal is accomplished, those who are able to heal find their value increased among their followers. And when the pain is gone, there is little concern for identifying who is the "real" healer. Fakes and charlatans get all mixed up with the sincere and genuine. In the eyes of those who have been delivered from pain, what man the healer does is on the same level as what God the Healer does.

Pentecostals assert that healing is of God. James' instruction to anoint with oil and pray for the sick (James 5:14) is the golden text of praying for the sick. God, who made man's body, soul, and spirit, has provided through Christ for the well-being of the whole man.

Honest John probably did not deserve his nickname. Folks who knew him rather supposed his list of sins was long, and he appeared to be adding to them—instead of subtracting.

But Honest John had a soft spot in his heart for preachers and churches. He even loved to talk religion during my occasional visits to his bargain store to search for church supplies.

"Say, Reverend, can you list the Ten Commandments in order?" might begin a discussion continuing until I backed out the door to the street.

One morning a sassy elderly lady, who in our small town had long since made known her dislike for Pentecostals, joined Honest John and me to make a threesome. She forthrightly launched an attack intended for an audience. Miraculous healings were on her mind this day, a phenomenon which she declared to be nonexistent.

In an attempt to hopefully bring the impending fracas to a speedy and peaceful conclusion, I simply bypassed theological arguments and stated that it had been my privilege to be present as an eyewitness to miracles of healing. There was a moment of silence, not long, which was broken by her caustic response: "Pshaw! That don't settle anything. I am twice as old as you are, and I have never seen anything like that."

While I was thinking of the distance between me and the peaceful street, Honest John drawled: "Ma'am, I reckon as how what you said don't settle anything. It only means you ain't been where he's been."

Procedure. Having a bottle of oil available for anointing the sick is a tradition in Pentecostal churches. Pure olive oil is commonly used (perhaps because it says "pure" and comes in hand-sized bottles). No power is ascribed to the oil itself. No prayers of exorcism and blessing are repeated over the oil by ministers. It is only symbolic of the power of the Holy Spirit. A study of the tabernacle in the wilderness of Sinai will reveal rich symbolism of oil representing the presence of the Holy Spirit. In addition, kings of Israel were anointed by prophets, and all high priests were anointed with oil (Exodus 30:22-33).

In Pentecostal churches the minister usually places oil on the forehead of the person desiring prayer. One or more people may place hands upon the head or shoulders, or hold the hands of the person desiring healing. One person may pray aloud, or the entire group may pray in concert.

In keeping with the command of Jesus Christ, prayer commonly includes the words "in the name of Jesus." In John 16:24 and other passages, Jesus taught that if petitions to heaven were asked in His name, the Father would hear and answer.

Miracles for Believers. While controversy regarding the authenticity of healing is a perpetual question among scholars, it is not a question among Pentecostals. Ask a gathering of believers if they have ever experienced or witnessed a divine healing, and the larger number will raise their hands affirmatively. Many will have personal stories to relate. In my own home, prayer for healing was (and is) as frequent as an illness or injury.

> *I saw a polio victim's braces removed and the girl of about age 12 take her first awkward steps since having been afflicted by the disease. Thousands were present at the event, which allowed verification that the girl had been paralyzed and that neither she, nor her family, had previously met the minister.*

One of the stronger arguments for explaining healings is that the illness was only psychological. However, it must be asserted that this argument fails largely for lack of evidence. After the healing there is no evidence to test, except improved health. And if healing the spirit heals the body, that too is a miracle.

Meanwhile, Pentecostals continue to practice what they believe. While they do not intend to live forever in the present world, they do believe that it is God's will for His people to enjoy a productive life. And to correct the ill effects of Adamic sin in our bodies, Jesus has provided for miraculous healing.

The fact that not every person prayed for is healed is only a semantic problem, not a theological one. That Jesus healed and gave power to heal is the theology of healing. That believers have been healed removes doubt. That sickness continues gives ample reason to keep trusting.

Divine healing, among Pentecostals and other religious groups, is a doctrine not likely to languish. Among Pentecostals, divine healing is a basic tenet of faith.

Eternal Life and Eternal Punishment

Pentecostals believe judgment is for eternity: an eternal reward of heaven awaits those who accept and follow Jesus Christ. Though hell was not designed for man, sin came through the fall of Adam. Those who choose to remain in sin and reject Jesus as Savior will spend eternity in a place of punishment, abysmally separated from the Creator God and His utopian paradise.

Life is the theme of faith, the essence of the Holy Spirit. After His water baptism, Jesus freely spoke of Himself as being life and the giver of life. There is no Christianity without Jesus. Without this Man from Nazareth, all that is called Christendom is undone, without purpose or meaning: He is the Christ of Christendom.

Christ taught that an acceptance of Him as the Son of God, the Messiah, would begin a born-again experience, symbolizing a new life. Being born again requires repentance for sins, asking God's forgiveness for those sins, and purposing to follow Jesus. The "old man" is the one who walked in sin; the "new man" is the one who chooses to follow Christ.

Therefore, to become a Christian is to die—to sin and to self. Physical living becomes second to life in the Spirit. Priorities are not just reordered: they are changed. A familiar saying to express this experience is "Born twice, die once; born once, die twice." This means that if a person (born of woman) is born again (born of Christ), his body will die but his spirit will never die (John 8:51). If a person (born of woman) never accepts Christ, he shall die twice (physically and through eternal separation from God).

Pentecostals believe those who die twice will spend an eternity in hell. Hell itself will be cast into the pit of death (lake of fire) on Judgment Day (Revelation 20:14). This is the second death.

The doctrine of eternal life and eternal punishment is firmly anchored in the teachings of Christ. No other writer or prophet in the Bible was as emphatic about eternal life being through faith in God as was Christ. Christ spoke with the greatest clarity about eternal death being where fire, darkness, and terror are without end.

The hope of eternal life is a driving force for the Christian pilgrim. *Fox's Book of Martyrs* is an excellent sourcebook of testimonies that the hope of living forever with Christ gave courage in time of death. This is more than a codification of rules of social living, or how to be nice to an enemy. Here is rested the fundamentals of the faith: Christ is the Resurrection! In Him, we live—eternally. Without Him, we die—eternally.

The Rapture and the Millennial Reign

Pentecostals believe that Jesus will gather to Himself the righteous living and dead, who will subsequently return to earth to reign with Him for a thousand years. After this millennial reign, they will spend an eternity together with Him in heaven.

Babel is the eternal story of man's desiring paradise and looking for a shortcut to get there. How to keep the good things of life and get rid of the bad is the question. No pain, no sorrow, no death, no old age . . . plenty of food and opportunities to enjoy leisure, travel, adventure. If such were true, there would be little or no interest in the hereafter. However, there could be no hereafter if the present offered no doors to the future.

Ancient man painted scenes of paradise on the walls of caves. Kings and pharaohs prepared burial sites with supplies to travel to lands beyond. Indians imagined lands in the sky where life was pleasant and hunting was bountiful.

Religions, both ancient and contemporary, offer hopes for the afterlife. Skeptics view the belief in an afterlife of the spirit as ranging from forms of mental illness to mystical beliefs that serve as shock absorbers for the tragedies of life.

Christians universally hold to belief in life after death. Heaven is a fixed idea of God and His people living together eternally. However, the process of getting to heaven, who gets to heaven, exactly when they get to heaven, where heaven is and what will happen in heaven—all are questions begging answers.

In Old Testament times, paradise (for believers) and hell (for unbelievers) were believed to be inside the earth. After Jesus' death, He took the saints of the Old Testament to a paradise above the earth. Most Christian theologies teach that since Christ's ascension, paradise for deceased believers is above.

Precisely when the soul goes above is a theological "hot potato." However, for Pentecostals there is no room for debate. There are only two alternatives.

The first alternative is death. When a believer dies, the spirit leaves the body, and the Bible suggests the believer's spirit is escorted by angels to a paradise above. At the resurrection of the righteous dead, the spirit will return to be reunited with the body—which will be a perfect body. The resurrection of the wicked will not be until after Jesus' 1,000-year reign on earth—called the millennial reign.

The other possibility for getting into the immediate presence of Jesus is the belief in the second coming of Christ. Conventionally called the Rapture, this belief is referred to as a "blessed hope" (Titus 2:13). When this event does occur, in a given moment every believer on earth will experience a momentary change of the physical body into a perfect body and rise up to be in the presence of the Lord (1 Corinthians 15:51, 52).

For Pentecostals, the evidence for the Rapture is overwhelming. Especially the Acts passage where angels appeared to Jesus' followers after the Ascension is believed to refer to the Rapture. "Ye men of Galilee, why stand ye gazing into heaven? this same Jesus, which is taken up from you into heaven, shall so come in like manner as ye have seen him go into heaven" (Acts 1:11).

Among the scriptures believed to speak specifically of the

Rapture are Luke 21:34-36; 1 Thessalonians 5:1-11; and 2 Thessalonians 2:6-8.

Evangelism: Reaching Lost Souls

"Go ye therefore, and teach all nations, baptizing them in the name of the Father, and of the Son, and of the Holy Ghost" (Matthew 28:19). Pentecostals believe that this mandate from Jesus Christ must be accomplished before His return to rapture His people away.

Because of the doctrine of the Rapture, Pentecostals intrinsically communicate a sense of urgency. Missionary efforts are predicated in a firm commitment that the Rapture is imminent. Every effort must be made to share the gospel of Christ with every man and woman on earth.

While the critics have sought to punch holes through the theology of the Rapture, the Pentecostals continue preaching it as an imminent event. The doctrine of the imminence of Christ's return is directly related to strong evangelism. The fledgling number of tongues-speakers of a hundred years ago has burgeoned to make Pentecostals one of the great forces of the religious world.

It is true that the question of when the Rapture is to take place has suffered some bruising. This event, which is not exclusive to Pentecostals, may be interpreted to precede the era of the Great Tribulation, be in the middle, or come at the end. Theologians in varied schools of thought disagree. Traditionally, Pentecostals have believed that the Rapture will precede God's wrath upon the wicked.[2] This will, of course, place

---

[2] In more recent years, "Kingdom" teaching and Charismatic influences have muted the belief in a pre-Tribulation coming of Christ for His church. Characteristically, high liturgical churches do not emphasize a time for Christ's return. Charismatics staying in high churches may simply dilute emphasis on the Rapture as a result of their exposure to negligent or antagonistic forces.

the righteous in the presence of the Lord, while the wicked are getting a taste of hell on earth.

A theological strain occurs, dividing Pentecostals from many other Christians who believe in the Rapture. Pentecostals see their primary mission until the Rapture as encouraging spiritual renewal by leading people to Christ. Being born again will divinely order one's social life, which fact is the surest and best way to a better world. The work of the eternal kingdom of Christ is the priority work of the believer.

Countering this approach are those who believe in the Rapture but strongly emphasize the role of human government. They insist that it is the God-given duty of man to use his talents and energies to shape human government for the coming of Christ. Pentecostals have traditionally had a tendency to minimize political involvement.

Meanwhile, the events in the Middle East and elsewhere are overwhelmingly supportive of prophetical teaching that has characterized Pentecostal churches. Until there are world events that openly refute prophetical teaching of Pentecostals of the past 100 years, Pentecostals are likely to continue to believe these are the last days and that the Rapture will soon occur.

If the Bible offers scriptures for the Rapture, and world events may be interpreted to corroborate these scriptures, the ball is in the Pentecostals' court. And for now they are playing very well.

CHAPTER 4

Myths Surrounding Pentecostals

▼ ▼ ▼ ▼ ▼ ▼ ▼ ▼ ▼ ▼ ▼ ▼

A lawyer's wife came by the church to bring a community bulletin. Knowing she was unacquainted with Pentecostals, I engaged her in conversation, during the course of which we were walking through the sanctuary. Suddenly, she froze.

"What is it?" I asked.

More candidly than she meant to answer, she quickly responded: "Oh, I don't know. This is just the first time that I have ever been in a Pentecostal church."

Myths may be honestly come by and believed to be the truth, but social damage caused by myths can be devastating. Over the years it has been my experience to have people flinch, withdraw, reflect fear, openly state anxiety, or take on an air of superiority when they became aware of a Pentecostal's presence.

In the earlier years of my life, it was extremely painful for me to experience being called "Holy Roller" or "one of them tongues people." It may well be that part of my drive to study sociology was to better understand both myself and the world around me, a world that tended to be very harsh and judgmental. Further, the world seemed willing to preserve the ignorance. My social class and intelligence were often deemed to be at the lower end of the scale. Achieving status was difficult. It required changing the preconceived ideas of folks who had already decided what Pentecostals and their children were supposed to be like. Their suppositions often translated into an obstacle course.

In the absence of truth, myths are easily constructed, perpetrated, and perpetuated. They may be innocent in nature or harmful, but the larger fact is that if they are believed, they do affect thinking and behavior. Whatever the origin and nature of myths, if they are believed, they are held to be truth. Myths may even become a part of a society's norms, thus inhibiting research.

Before proceeding with particular myths, it is fair to point out that all religions are negatively affected to some extent by myths. Those who adhere to any faith imply exclusivism to those not of that faith. This exclusivism is naturally interpreted as a certain social distance or elitism giving variant qualitative values or social worth to humans. The end result is that a hierarchy of social structure leaves those not members of the group in the larger and lower part of the pyramid. In effect, those not like us are not as good or as right as we are. Pity, sympathy, compassion, generosity, anger, violence, hatred, disdain, and indifference represent an admixture of feelings, attitudes, and behaviors toward those perceived to differ from one's group of orientation.

Pentecostals believe in a work of grace in addition to salvation. Being baptized with the Holy Spirit may occur at the same time as salvation or later, but it is a distinctly different work of grace than salvation. This heavenly blessing is available for all Christians, but not received by all. A person who is not a Christian cannot experience this work of grace. However, grace for salvation is available to all, after which every believer is a candidate for the Holy Spirit baptism.

What results is an exclusivism. Exclusivism is social dynamite, separating the *haves* from the *have-nots*. Thus it is not only true but also predictable and logical that Pentecostals are accused of things they sometimes have never even heard of, much less have fallen into the error of doing.

It is therefore fitting to deal with myths. In the reality of life, myths may have greater force than does the truth. If folks believe the myth, it is not a myth to them, but the truth. Myths may be of greater import in forming opinions, values, and behavior than irrefutable facts that are obvious but not believed.

This is not to suggest that the following myths concerning Pentecostals are inclusive. They simply represent the more common ones associated with Pentecostals.

Myth 1: All Tongues-Speakers Are Alike

We were sitting in a posh conference room of an attorney's office. Our purpose was a million-dollar business transaction for a charity organization in which we all ostensibly had a mutual interest. Friendships among those present did exist, but my relationship was between cordial and professional, having been nurtured by only a few formal meetings. The history of our discussions had clearly charted a path that left a consciousness in the air that all others present were from different church backgrounds.

Twenty years earlier, whether such a meeting would have been possible is questionable. Theological distance would have prevented such social togetherness. But changing times and common need had drawn us together; and, while our perspectives were divergent, our goal was singular.

Having negotiated some difficult terrain with the agenda, we approached adjournment. In an attempt to lighten the atmosphere, a well-intentioned member turned to me and said:

"Well, Harold, I must say that I am impressed with you. I have told my wife and daughter about you, and they are looking forward to meeting a real, live Holy Roller."

He and the rest of the members laughed, the sort of laugh that begrudgingly extends fraternity yet concedes anxiety.

I forced myself to smile and prayed for the Holy

> *Spirit to touch me, for I knew that in their minds I was like an aborigine getting a Ph.D. There was silence in anticipation of my response.*
>
> *It was my rite of passage into their social graces. Sitting beside the good-natured architect who had proffered condescending friendship, I simply leaned in his direction, slid my right hand down into my suit pocket, acted as if I were trying to scoop something into my hand, and said, "Frank, would you like to see my snake?"*

God formed us by His hand in our mother's womb (Job 31:15; Psalm 139:13). Individuality is a characteristic of premium importance in every aspect of life. Blessings of God are upon individuals and complement God-given gifts and talent.

Are all Pentecostals the same? Popular literature suggests a generic yes. But to read the literature is to readily understand that the authors, whether or not they mean well, often lack intimate knowledge of the diversity in the camp of the Pentecostals.

Lack of research is an issue. The difficulty of accurate reporting is compounded by the tendency to deal with unusual, bizarre, or negative experiences. Thus, individuals living happy, productive, nonpublic, nondramatic lives escape the scrutiny and pen of the reporters and popular writers.

Tongues is that factor which most intrigues, fascinates, frustrates, angers, or causes fear of Pentecostals. It is the phenomenon that distinctively sets apart the Pentecostal from other Christian churches. In practice, the belief is that when a Christian is baptized with the Holy Spirit, he is divinely empowered to speak a heavenly language.

All Christians who have received the Holy Spirit and speak in tongues stand in common proof that Acts 2 is applicable to the 20th century. Exactly how to receive tongues, the responsibility and the use of tongues, and the lifestyle of the believer are arenas of controversy.

For the better part of the last 100 years, a few denominations carried the weight of the fresh new move of the Holy Spirit. The Church of God dates its beginning to 1886 in the western hills of North Carolina. The Assemblies of God had West Coast origins in the Azusa Street revival of 1906. Pentecostal Holiness, the Church of God of Prophecy, Foursquare, Church of God in Christ, and other denominations also have developed strong organizations emphasizing their Pentecostal orientation.

An essential part of the doctrine of the Holy Spirit is that it cannot be contained by a man or a denomination. As preachers and laypeople moved across America, revivals affected whole communities. In the North Carolina city of Gastonia, the revival reached such proportions that factories were closed for workers to attend the meetings.

Miracles were the order of the day. Social misfits, callous sinners, and people of every type and description came to hear and see what would happen. Folks were saved from their sins, healed, delivered from vile habits, and filled with the Holy Spirit. Fellowship bodies formed and churches were established.

Those who set out to harm preachers and churches often found an altar of prayer instead. Fires set by arsonists to burn churches and tents miraculously did not burn. And there were reports of folks, "in the Spirit," picking up hot coals of fire and not being burned. Alcoholics were freed from their habit. Healings were common.

Many of the myths that have plagued Pentecostals are founded in those days of revivals. The unusual draws the strange and bizarre along with the honest and sincere. The curious, idle, and mischievous all came to be a part of the revivals, often attempting disruption or harm. Stories of divine intervention abound:

> People would fall under the power all over the tent. I well remember one man who got up in a tree near the altar so he could see the people in the altar. The power struck him and he fell to the ground crying for mercy. . . .

> Gambling houses, poolrooms, and church ice-cream sup-
> pers were closed out. . . . Sometimes over a hundred hungry
> souls would make a rush to the altar and commence crying
> to God.[1]

And the wealthy began to take notice. For example, in Kan-
napolis, North Carolina, a Pentecostal congregation so powerful-
ly moved a town with prayer, revival, and born-again experiences that the founder of Cannon Mills favored the local congregation with generous gifts. Land was provided for a church and
orphanage, both of which exist to this day.

However, individuals possessing wealth or having excellent
education were rare in the movement. Even so, their presence
and leadership abilities were widely respected. Willingness to
be guided by these leaders is a further refutation of the anti-
intellectual bias attributed to the movement.[2]

All social factors combined, the end result was that most of
these early churches were either in the poorer parts of towns and
cities or in the country. "The church across the tracks" became
derogatory terminology commonly used by critics until recent
decades to refer to Pentecostal churches.

Purchase of premium land was often limited by finances.
Folks do not generally tend to locate in communities inconsis-
tent with their social class. Hardship forced the purchase of land
consistent with budget. Though it seemed reasonable at the time
to buy such land, the stigma of Pentecostals' poverty early in the
history of the movement is so painful that many Pentecostal
ministers still flinch at the mention of it.

Facts are facts. There is no defense against the observation
that the current Pentecostal Movement was founded among

---

[1] J. W. Buckalew, *Incidents in the Life of J. W. Buckalew* (Cleveland, Tennessee:
Church of God Publishing House, n.d.), pp. 122-124. Cited in Conn, p. 108.

[2] Conn, pp. 52-53.

lower socioeconomic groups. It needs no defense, only explanation.

The poor are God's people. Jesus' ministry reached with compassion to touch the poor, to heal them, and to invite them to become part of His kingdom. Let it be said that there is a great deal of difference between being poor and being sorry. Honest, hardworking folks have dignity. And even those poor without dignity have a right to the gospel.

It is no marvel that the Pentecostal revival broke out among the lower classes. Grass-roots revivals traditionally have been without the masthead that attracts the elite. The upper classes have ever tended to have their own agenda. Vested interest in society inherently prohibits investing in movements that threaten the status quo.

Discussion of social class is not complete without recognizing the steady upward mobility of members of the movement. Explanations are numerous. Better times is a logical one, but it does not naturally fit. If the poor foster a cycle of poverty, then an answer for upward mobility must be more concrete, more credible than better economic times. Better education is a plausible theory, thus increasing job opportunities and income. Improved roads and communications have created greater access to the marketplaces, thus even the poor are more cosmopolitan.

There is another answer for why Pentecostals have progressively moved toward the middle class. Their religious ethos encouraged hard work, not being wasteful but saving, and going to church. Much in the tradition of the original Methodists, Pentecostals' simple lifestyle and rejection of expensive pleasures enabled the accumulation of material goods. Improved economics and changing times combined to facilitate better education for children. These factors together contributed to upward mobility. All of this, quite naturally, was considered a heavenly blessing.

The issue of cloning Pentecostals has never approached reality. To share common social or religious beliefs and practices does not equate replication. The letters of the apostle Paul clearly chart a path of unity in diversity. He wrote of each having different gifts of the Holy Spirit, but asserted that "we, being many, are one body in Christ" (Romans 12:4-6). He used the analogy of the human body: Different members of the body make one person. But who would argue that a hand and a foot are the same thing? Each is an entity with certain potential, but the greater use of either is when there is interdependency.

It is not unusual for a local Pentecostal congregation to be comprised of members from backgrounds of diverse denominations. Other members may have been previously unaffiliated with any church. Preferences for worship techniques may vary as widely as the different perspectives on how to govern a local church. Worship services further highlight these differences as individuals decide seriatim whether to participate in any given part of worship, for example, concert prayer, and clapping of hands. Tolerance is generous, allowing each individual the choice of participating or observing.

Finally, the question of whether all tongues-speakers are alike can be addressed by personalities. Rex Humbard (Independent), David Bennett (Episcopalian), Edward O'Connor (Roman Catholic), Pat Robertson (Southern Baptist), Vinson Synan (Pentecostal Holiness), and John Gunstone (Anglican) all claim the blessing of being Spirit-filled and tongues-speakers. All are leaders among tongues-speakers. What a presumption it is to suggest that they are all alike. Neither are their followers alike. They simply share a common experience.

Myth 2: All Pentecostals Speak in Tongues

They called me a Pentecostal in school and on the playground. In truth, I was not even a Christian. Dad said we weren't Christian until we chose to be born again, which I did not do until I was 14.

My adoption into the body of believers was accepted solely on my testimony of receiving Jesus Christ as my personal Lord. The experience of speaking in other tongues did not happen for me at the time of salvation, which was a disappointment.

No adventurer ever set off on a safari with greater determination than I set out to receive the gift of the Holy Spirit baptism. A good number of believers who had received the gift took a personal and avid interest in my hopeful success. As often as there was an opportunity to resort to the altar of a church, whether at home or away, my earnest prayer was a petition to be baptized with the Holy Spirit and thereby receive the ability to speak in other tongues.

This pilgrimage lasted for about five years, with countless trips to the altar. Defeat was not an issue; neither was there the thought that it would not happen. Besides, all along the way, I witnessed many receive the baptism of the Holy Spirit and speak in tongues. Doubt as to the validity of the experience was not a question, but I was chagrined when new converts spoke in other tongues. There was the feeling of being passed up by a novice.

Such a lengthy journey took me past a variety of techniques and methods. Folks have their own ideas about most things, and there seemed to be an un-countable number of ideas about how to receive the Holy Spirit. A good number of these seemed suffi-ciently palatable to be attempted—that which was desired was worth investment.

After five years of being a born-again Christian and not being baptized with the Holy Spirit, I had explored or rejected most of the techniques. My rou-tine was back to a rather basic GO-TO-THE-TOP-AND-PRAYERFULLY-ASK-GOD-FOR-WHAT-YOU-WANT.

Certainly, I would be remiss not to mark progress during these years. Bit by bit my prayer life strength-ened me to give up habits, little and big, that were not

Christlike and to begin forming ways and thoughts more like Christ. A tendency to measure my progress by the pace of others was thwarted. My ambitions were molded into plans with greater care for others.

More often than not, when leaving the altar during those five years, I felt the Holy Spirit gently prod me to make amends and restitution or to reprogram my thoughts and habits.

Finally, sitting in a college convocation at the age of 19, I felt a quiet resolve to go to the altar and stay there until I was filled with the Holy Spirit. Fasting and praying had brought me to a point of knowing that I could not do the work of Christ, as He had called me, without the power of the Holy Spirit in my life.

Only minutes after kneeling and beginning to pray, I experienced the pleasantness and sweetness of the Holy Spirit as I never had before. I began to verbally, but softly, give praise to God for what I knew was happening.

Suddenly to my mind came the question "What about the tongues?" To my delight a language I had never spoken began to flow from my lips. Totally coherent, it was my choice to utter the flow of sounds which came to my mind. I did, and the joy was worth all of the searching and seeking . . . and it still is.

That September night of my 19th year, I really became a practicing Pentecostal—something I had been called all my life.

Begin with basic research. Get the doctrinal statements of Protestant churches, the Roman Catholic Church, and the Greek Orthodox Church. Like a thread running through a magnificent tapestry, there will be a common acceptance that the biblical account of Acts 2 is true. That it has variant interpretations does not detract from its validity.

By and large, Christian churches talk freely about the Holy

Spirit and the power of the Holy Spirit. Among these churches, speaking in tongues in Acts is generally accepted as being divinely ordered to assist in evangelizing the world in New Testament times.

Christians who received the latter-day outpouring of the baptism of the Holy Spirit with the evidence of speaking in other tongues quickly came to be known as "tongues people." Churches organized by these "tongues people," who did not find acceptance in their own churches, were called Pentecostal churches. The name is specifically associated with the Acts 2 experience.

It is critically important to understand that the word Pentecostal, as it refers to a particular people, is relatively new in usage. While history is replete with accounts of Christians filled with the Holy Spirit and speaking in tongues, it has only been in the last century that the name Pentecostal has come to designate a particular group of people or certain denominations. Around the turn of the 20th century, the terminology was intended more for specifying individuals or small groups than denominations. No mainstream denomination in the United States emphasized the baptism of the Holy Spirit as a separate work of grace, with speaking in other tongues as a witness of such baptism.

Church buildings, most humble in location and appearance, were constructed, purchased, or converted to serve growing numbers. Fledgling congregations began to grapple with their identity. While heavenly blessings were being received, earthly woes took their toll. Preachers were stoned and jailed, churches were burned, and members were denied credit by individuals and businesses who resented Pentecostals.

> *As late as the 1970s this author was faced with a city manager who controlled building permits and was reluctant to grant a permit to Pentecostals. He openly said that Pentecostals ought to "get out of town into the woods in the country, where they belong."*

The opposition to and persecution of Pentecostals in the early part of this century only served to fan the fervency of the revival and the determination of the tongues-speakers. No fire motivates zealots like opposition; it is the proof of truth and the call for sacrifice. In the spirit of the Day of Pentecost, the Holy Spirit moved revivalists from city to city, state to state, and country to country.

Sinners were saved, and the saved accepted and received the baptism of the Holy Spirit. Families gathered for worship. Certain characteristics conspicuously described Pentecostals, and strong emphasis on the family was one of them. High value was placed on families worshiping together at home and at church.

Sometimes only one person in a family would claim the experience of speaking in tongues, but the entire family would attend the Pentecostal church. The logical result was that the community called all members of the family "Pentecostals." The word in conventional usage became more a cultural definition than a theological term.

Many nominal churches practice infant baptism, purporting to bring each child into the family of God and into the fellowship of the local church. This tradition of the Roman Catholic Church has progressively become a practice of many Protestants since Martin Luther. To baptize an infant in water presumably makes it a permanent member of the body of Christ.

The practice of infant baptism is not acceptable to Pentecostals. Children must be old enough to personally acknowledge Christ as their Savior before they may become a member of a Pentecostal church. Equally, the privilege of membership does not require the believer to speak in other tongues.

No mainstream Pentecostal church advocates that the experience of tongues is a prerequisite for heaven. Salvation is solely by the unmerited favor of God and based on confession of sins and acceptance of Christ. There is no exclusivism. Every Christian is eligible to receive the baptism of the Holy Spirit and speak in tongues.

There is no gigantic division of fellowship between Christians who do speak in tongues and those who do not. All are brothers and sisters in Christ. All are considered equally saved, though certain positions in leadership structure may require affirmation of having been baptized with the Holy Spirit and speaking in other tongues.

If "Pentecostal" is understood as a church or body of people, it is appropriate to call those who attend such fellowships "Pentecostals." This would even include those non-Christians who prefer, for whatever reasons and with whatever regularity, to attend Pentecostal churches.

If the word *Pentecostal* is used to refer to the experience of Acts, then not all those who attend Pentecostal churches can be called Pentecostals. In practice, those who attend Pentecostal churches are called Pentecostals, though many who call themselves Pentecostals make no claim to speaking in other tongues.

One Pentecostal denomination found in a survey that only 45 percent of the members testified to speaking in tongues.[3] Nonmembers and unbelievers who attended were not included in the survey.

There is a fringe element of those who have no direct association with any local church but would list their preference of religion as "Pentecostal." For example, upon entering a hospital, nursing home, the military, and so forth, individuals may be asked their religious preference. Their stated preference can by no means be assumed to be an indication of attendance, fellowship, or practice of Pentecostalism.

It is a simple definition to say that Pentecostals are those who speak in tongues and attend Pentecostal churches. But how to properly define family, friends, and acquaintances who have roots in Pentecostalism, attend a Pentecostal church but do not

---

[3] Survey of Church of God, Cleveland, Tennessee, 1986.

speak in tongues or do not believe in tongues, or who speak in tongues but don't attend a Pentecostal church is a large question. Unfortunately, popular literature tends to blend categories that may not be compatible, thus representing community where it does not exist. Those not knowledgeable of Pentecostals are left with only a bird's-eye view of a complex question.

Myth 3: Pentecostals Are Too Emotional

When she stepped into the sanctuary, she had presence. Her carriage was that of royalty, suggesting not less than a genteel life of affordable leisure. With cautious dignity she proceeded to the third pew in front of the altar and gracefully sat down.

The singing was spirited and lively. Completely surrounding her were voices heartily sounding praises. To all of this she was stoical.

Then it happened. To her right a person began to clap his hands. I saw her face. For just a moment there was panic. She furtively glanced in the direction of this new phenomenon, without turning her head, as if to ensure that there was no danger. Then she quickly regained her composure, as though relieved that all was safe.

Sunday after Sunday she returned. Her place in the pew was always the same as the first visit—only some 20 feet in front of the pastor's chair. She sat, stood, knelt, listened—all with the decorum of her stately initial entrance.

"Could it be true?" I asked myself one Sunday morning as I looked in her direction during the praise and worship time. To my amazement, her hands were moving silently through the air, as if to clap. However, the hands never touched—always staying about six inches apart.

As the Sundays passed, her motions became more fluid, more natural, less inhibited. In time the hands were touching, softly, and the rhythm was in keeping with the music.

One evening as we talked in the parlor of her home, she said to me:

"I don't know where I have been all my 67 years, though I have been in church all my life. But wherever I have been, there were lots of other people with me.

"What I have experienced in this church is a new and more wonderful way of life than I have ever known. I always believed in God. But for the first time in my life, I feel God's personal love for me."

A major indictment against Pentecostals is that emotionalism is the primary focus of worship. The implication, or innuendo, is that Pentecostals are practicing a primitive religion, finding release for life's frustrations in physical exercises. Stories told of Pentecostals range from the amusing to the ridiculous, and may or may not contain a grain of truth.

What must be remembered is that two facts are here being explored. First is the myth of too much emotionalism among Pentecostals. Second is the myth of the behaviors associated with the emotionalism.

Emotions are a natural part of man. Pentecostals do not spend great amounts of time compartmentalizing life. Life is a package. It is wrapped and tied up together. Religion pervades life, and life finds its essence in worship and service to God. The equation begets a fullness of joy that includes the right to physical and verbal expression of worship and praise.

At issue is not whether man is entitled to be emotional but what the proper display of those emotions is, as well as when and where these feelings should be expressed or demonstrated. It is only when etiquette, format, and procedure become the god of religion that the discussion is frustrated.

Pentecostals may clap their hands, pat their feet, say "Amen," sway, or even happily jump up and down. It is not true that such behavior is required, or even the norm. Neither is it true that those who fail to do these things are necessarily criticized, stigmatized, or ostracized. Nor is it true that worship responses can be predicted from service to service, or from church to church.

The paradox of the emotional issue is that all the things Pentecostals do in worship are normal social behaviors. No psychologist would find need of treatment for the emotional manifestations that occur in Pentecostal worship if they happened in a context other than church.

The Other Side. Churches that tend to follow liturgies are referred to by various names, but a commonly accepted term is *High Church.* Worship has been routinized with events made sacred by tradition. Symbolism is extensive, with every act, object, and color relating to theology or culture. Ministers and others trained to carry out the worship activities lead, while the congregation observes or participates as requested or permitted by the leaders.

The consequence is that creativity by individuals is discouraged in a liturgical setting. The congregation acts as a body to perform worship in keeping with established practices. The predication is that the more appropriately rituals and liturgies are followed, the higher the sense of spiritual fulfillment experienced by the worshipers. Tradition is sacred. Contrariwise, to depart from established tradition is to profane the sacred.

Effectively, liturgical churches do not cultivate or create opportunities for individual expression in worship, or so a Pentecostal would argue. In addition, liturgical churches are favored by society as the official representatives of God when society needs such a representation. A certain co-optation results in which the liturgical churches tend to develop worship, practices, and beliefs which, if not congruent with the secular society, at least are not opposed to the ideas of public leaders.

The sociology of this is understandable. Public leaders represent pluralism. Religion has the potential to be politically controversial. When public leaders need a religious application, they must be certain that the person will perform predictably. Churches that have provided written prayers, sermons, and speeches for ministers ensure uniformity. In addition, most public leaders have roots in or greater awareness of nominal churches.

The Pentecostal Perspective. To the Pentecostal minister, ritualization of the gospel is compromise. While the gospel is unchangeable, its application must be personalized, as the Holy Spirit directs the individual's life. However, the penalty is that Pentecostals are considered unpredictable and not properly ecumenical. Therefore, they are rarely asked to share public forums. Whatever the reasons for the absence of certain religious leaders from public agendas, it cannot be construed as irrelevant or incidental. There are valid sociological reasons to explain which religious leaders are selected for public office.

Pentecostals do not have the accumulation of centuries of tradition. This may well contribute to the explanation of why their thought and practice have an orientation differing from liturgical churches. The will of God is the only will by which man should live and worship. Worship is not to be a ritual, tradition, or custom.

The commandment objecting to idols is effective to keep Pentecostal churches relatively free of icons. Dependence on physical objects or ritualistic acts is perceived to range from spiritual immaturity to paganism. "God is Spirit, and those who worship Him must worship in spirit and truth" (John 4:24, *NKJV*).

Truth without deviation has reference to knowledge of the Bible, thus knowledge of God. From the time of acceptance of Christ by the individual, daily Bible reading and prayer are emphasized as a way of life. Bible studies in the church and homes are a religious act.

A host of "stars" have passed through the Pentecostal ranks. Fancy buses, flashy clothes, and even fees for speaking mark their lifestyle. However, popularity without character tends to have a short lifespan. And stardom is difficult, if not impossible, to attain when Jesus is the primary focus.

Pentecostals do not find their thrills in recounting past sins, telling of their exploits, or planning how to even scores with the devil or those who belong to the devil. The excitement of being a Pentecostal is clearly anchored in what Christ has done and will do and the hope of eternal life with Christ. Blessings experienced in daily living are carried into worship as gifts of praise to God. The cord connecting faith and works is inseparable. We believe. God does. We praise God.

Self-expression in worship is then welcomed. Thankful people give thanks, and they give thanks particularly. Praise is right, proper, and in keeping with the Pentecostals' understanding of how it will be in heaven, where praises to God are eternal.

To make a disposition of the issue of emotional and physical expression in worship, it must be reiterated that acceptable expression in Pentecostal worship is within normal limits of social and mental behavior. The myth of excess is a consequence of lack of accurate knowledge of actual events and a lack of understanding of the theological base of Pentecostal worship.

It is human nature to fear that which we do not understand. Those in churches who feel Pentecostals are newcomers on the block quite naturally misunderstand the emotional worship practices of Pentecostals. But it is also notable that they have never been part of Pentecostal worship, nor have they read literature authored by Pentecostals.

Ironically, current trends indicate that a large percentage of the growth among Pentecostals has been from people leaving the "higher churches" in search of individualism in worship. In a world which emphasizes individuality, it may be that people are looking for worship where personal expression is valued.

Myth 4: Pentecostals Use "Holy Powders" and Snakes

As a new pastor, I once referred in a message to the myth of "holy powders." A young man from a nominal church later explained to me that he had immediately moved away from the aisle in fear that "holy powders" would be cast upon him. While we laughed about it (after he realized there is no such potion), it has since been a reminder to me of the power of fear resulting from wrong accusations.

No evidence is necessary to fuel a myth. In fact, the denial of a myth may be the most certain method of ensuring that it continues. This writer, in hopes of relieving ignorance, may only fuel the fire of the myth of "holy powders" and that all Pentecostals handle snakes. However, the hope is that this explanation will correct error instead.

While teaching junior high in the early 1970s, I overheard two of my students talking about a local church. "Really?" I asked the girls. "Tell me more about this church and the things they do."

With certainty that presumed more than imagination, the girls shared how people would gather in the building, turn out the lights, dance themselves into a frenzy, and then lie around on the floor exhausted. In the quasi-darkness the minister would walk among the bodies, lay his hands on them, and say powerful religious words (whether of God or the devil was not clear).

When the spellbinding story was completed, I asked where this church was located. This they readily shared, though they appeared quite frightful should any of the believers ever learn that they knew of the secret doings.

"Girls," I said, "you really should be more careful. Have either of you ever been to this church of which you speak?" They shook their heads negatively.

I responded: "I have been on several occasions. In fact, I know the pastor quite well—he's my dad."

Several years later it was my privilege to perform the wedding ceremony for one of the girls in the preceding story. The event took place in the very church that had been implicated in the conversation.

It has been said that Pentecostals use "holy powders" to incite emotional ecstasies. Supposedly, a form of magical powders is secretly sprinkled on those who come to worship, and the effect is loss of reason followed by convulsions, contortions, and gyrations that would be the envy of a calisthenics coach. The myth holds that physical antics are an integral part of a spiritual experience.

In circulating freely among Pentecostals, never have I seen or even been privy to conversation regarding "holy powders." As an ordained minister of a mainstream Pentecostal church, my professional and informal training have never included the words or reference to "holy powders," except in Bible-school days when we students laughed at the ridiculousness of the idea. And, it should be said, in over 20 years of preparation for and service in the ministry, never have I heard "shoptalk" among Pentecostals that included or gave credence to "holy powders."

But "holy powders" is only suggestive of the seriousness of harmful myths. "Holy Rollers," as Pentecostals were once referred to in slang language, are subject to accusations that they use whatever techniques and/or tools necessary to generate a certain level of frenzy. The frenzy is theorized by critics as being the necessary emotional release to enable Pentecostals to maintain a level of social functionality. This too is a myth.

While teaching college and pastoring a southwestern Virginia congregation, I was frequently asked whether our congregation handled snakes. Finally, in protest, I asked a certain accuser: "What kind of snakes?"

Thinking he had indeed met a real, live snake-handler, he stammeringly repeated, "Just snakes."

Not willing to let him off so easily, I persisted. "Be specific; rattlesnakes, copperheads . . . what kind of snakes?"

To this he very nervously answered, "Rattlesnakes," and I had the feeling he expected to see one any second.

"Oh, no," I objected. "We haven't had anyone bitten in so long that it is getting dull and boring. But we do have a shipment of king cobras coming in Saturday night. Why don't you come over and visit with us?"

When he realized the absurdity of his question, my answer, and my total fear of snakes (big and small), he was amply embarrassed. We laughed together.

For Pentecostals who have been denied friendship, social access, and business dealings because of the myth of snake-handling, there is no room for humor. Most often the myth causes rejection without the Pentecostals' being aware or having the slightest opportunity to address the problem.

One of the most popular myths concerning Pentecostals is that they are snake-handlers. In all my life of experiencing worship an average of better than three times each week in Pentecostal churches, I have never seen snakes in a church. I have never known a minister or congregation that handled snakes. I have never even talked with anyone who has shared with me that he has been in a church service where there were snakes.

It is true by public records that there are some independent and small bodies of people who call themselves Pentecostals that include snake-handling as a part of their demonstration of faith. However, no official of any major Pentecostal organization, to my knowledge, endorses the practice of handling snakes.

Research indicates that the leading Pentecostal denominations in America have never adopted dogma or doctrine favoring the testing of faith by handling snakes. For any minister in such denominations as Church of God, Assemblies of God, Pentecostal Holiness, and Foursquare to even intimate approval for snake-handling would result in severe sanctions.

A plausible explanation as to why the myth exists rests in the syndication of newspaper articles about those (part of a cultist group) who call themselves Pentecostals and do practice snake-handling. Folks who read or hear news reports about alleged snake-handling among "Pentecostals" thus assume a direct relationship between the two, especially if they are ignorant of mainstream Pentecostalism. To charge that a Pentecostal handling a snake means all Pentecostals handle snakes would be as foolish as saying some snake-handlers are men and therefore all men handle snakes.

For the record, all of the confusion regarding this myth has two scriptural references. The first is found in Mark 16:18: "They shall take up serpents. . . ." The second reference is in Acts 28:4, 5, where Paul, apparently bitten by a deadly snake, threw it off and acted as if nothing had happened.

Mainstream Pentecostals believe that the Mark and Acts references indicate the protective hand of God in dangerous situations, protection that is still possible for us today.[4] However, by no means should this be used as a basis to invite danger into our lives. To the contrary, Ecclesiastes 7:17 is an appropriate positional statement guiding Pentecostals in all matters in which a Christian is faced with danger: "Neither be thou foolish: why shouldest thou die before thy time?" Since life is precious and a gift of God, no person should ever frivolously invite harm or death in a senseless conflict.

To accuse all Pentecostals of being snake-handlers because a few isolated, independent congregations handle snakes is gross ignorance. Various cults in the world consider certain snakes sacred, or instruments for worship. They must be studied and understood within their own context. To simply say "Pentecostals

---

[4]This treatise makes no attempt to explain the peculiar beliefs and practices of independent Pentecostal churches which to this day reportedly handle snakes.

handle snakes" is to exhibit the same intelligence level as asserting that all Episcopalians are homosexuals because a northern New Jersey group of Episcopalians voted in 1988 that marriages between homosexuals are blessed of God.

Can the myth of Pentecostals' handling snakes be debunked? Probably not. It is too easily fueled. It is tangible, allowing easy visual images. Even if years of efforts were put into public relations to correct this myth, one newspaper article with a picture of some small, isolated group could easily reverse the progress. Probably, attempts to eradicate the myth of snake-handling only fuel the issue.

The greater misfortune is that millions of Pentecostals are penalized by the myth of snake-handling. The silent judgment is deadly, since the person accused is often unaware of the charge. Friendships and relationships are handled on a qualitative basis assuming the myth to be true. In other cases, personal relationships are forfeited because of beliefs that snakes are handled. In essence, there are those people who do not even proffer friendship or fellowship with Pentecostals because of fear rooted in myths.

So, Pentecostals continue to bear the stigma of the snake-handling myth, even when it is considered to be a sin and absolutely abhorred by mainstream Pentecostals.

Myth 5: Pentecostals Are Antieducation

In an attempt to supplement our family income while pastoring a small church, it seemed logical to apply for a faculty position at the local community college. The dean of instruction, a friend of mine, had indicated a shortage of part-time instructors. At his encouragement, I placed an application on file.

After an inordinate delay of several weeks, an administrative official of the college shared with me that my application had not been approved.

Reportedly, one of the top five administrators was strongly opposed. Countering this open opposition was another official of the college who was equally determined to win approval. Though the opposition had failed to "blackball" my appointment, the application had become a thorny issue dividing the leadership of the college.

In an attempt to resolve the matter, the president of the college called a meeting to review the case. The professor opposing my appointment raised the following objection.

"Do you think that a person of this applicant's religious persuasion has the mental capability to function on the college level?"

The quote above is virtually verbatim, according to an administrative official who was present in the meeting. My redemption arrived via the fact that my studies included a master's degree from The College of William and Mary. I had entered this prestigious state school without any credit deficiencies from the bachelor of arts program I had completed at Lee College, a Church of God liberal arts college. Further, the acute shortage of teachers at the community college seemed to necessitate my being given a chance.

Not once was I allowed to defend my credentials, experience, or character. Nor was I asked to explain my religious beliefs, either to validate or reject the anxieties of my opponents. Persons non-Christian, agnostic, atheistic, and humanistic were employed. My employment was opposed on nonacademic grounds. It was indeed ironic that within an academic setting there should be the denial of academic discourse. But prejudice, by its very nature, denies scholarship. I was being seen first as a Pentecostal, second as a person, and third as a scholar.

Not until after I was employed by the college was the above story related to me in its full context. It was received with humor and has been good for many a wry smile in retrospection. Nevertheless, it brought me full abreast of the fact that many doors of opportunity in my life would be closed by prejudice—

and perhaps without my awareness.

Response. Pentecost was not birthed in halls of ivy. It is not at the heart a scholar's respite. It does not inherently cultivate debates, seminars, and think tanks. Its primary purpose is not the assimilating of cognitive knowledge or the discovery of new knowledge.

Pentecost, as described in its original setting of Acts 2, did not include even one noted scholar of the times. However, if a noted scholar was indeed present in the Upper Room, it is certain he was filled with the Holy Spirit and spoke with other tongues: "And they were *all* filled with the Holy Ghost, and began to speak with other tongues" (v. 4).

The Pentecostal Movement, dating to the late 1800s, similarly was not born in an academic setting. It must be carefully noted, however, that an event's occurrence outside a formal academic setting does not mean it is nonacademic. The discovery of existing knowledge is a separate phenomenon from that of creating and assimilating new knowledge.

The gospel of Jesus Christ is existing knowledge. By its very nature it is missionary, and the doctrines related to Pentecost are fundamentally related to spreading the gospel. Pentecost is a component of the gospel. It is not an emphasis on itself, or a glorifying of its own virtues. It is not a beginning of anything new, or a launching of different emphases.

Pentecost is nothing less and nothing more than the Holy Spirit's being sent from heaven to equip believers to do the work of Christ. The purpose and scope of the Holy Spirit are mandated to continue and complete the work of building and caring for Christ's church on earth.

A phenomenon that does not exist to itself cannot be isolated to itself without stagnation and deterioration. To isolate the Holy Spirit into an academic setting is to defeat His essence. He cannot be separated from the task He has been commissioned to effect. Pentecost is not a positing of an intellectual idea but the delivery of a force, a power to carry out a mandate: to share the good news of Jesus Christ as the Savior of the world.

Conflict Is Unavoidable. God, who made all things, knows all things, sees all things, and has all wisdom, gives to Christians the Holy Spirit. Christians are charged to accept by faith the sovereignty of God and to militantly, in a spiritual sense, share this faith with non-Christians. The Bible is the ultimate guidebook for understanding how to be a Christian and how to carry out the process of sharing faith.

Every Christian is charged to be knowledgeable of the Bible. "Study to shew thyself approved unto God" (2 Timothy 2:15) is a mandate to believers. Failure to study the Bible has sanctions. God no longer "winks at" ignorance (Acts 17:30). Sins of ignorance are in the same category as willful sins. Sins of omission are as serious as sins of commission (James 4:17).

However, no mention is made in Scripture of awards or rewards to be given on Judgment Day specifically to scholars. There simply is no logical argument, either in the life of Christ or in the writings of His apostles, that places high premiums on being an intellectual. To the contrary, all class symbols are eliminated, with the ground being level at the Cross. Those who reach the highest sainthood are to be the servants of others.

Paul wrote of himself that he feared lest he "should be a castaway" (1 Corinthians 9:27), even after he had virtually crisscrossed the known world telling the good news of Jesus Christ. Paul is one of the most scholarly of the canonical writers. His admonishments to Timothy resound with encouragement to study the Word.

Scholarship, in and of itself, is not a key to heaven. Scholarship follows in the wake of a commitment to Jesus Christ. It is primarily motivated by a desire to be more like Christ, and a better witness for Christ.

Christians who pursue higher education must do so with the purest of motives. Servanthood in Christ's church is the key principle. The place where one studies, and the nature of those studies, must be carefully charted through prayer and the working out of one's commitment to Christ. Education primarily for personal gain or fame is carnal. Every believer is an instrument in the hands of the Holy Spirit to be used as a witness and laborer in the church.

While this is a paradox for non-Christians, it is not a conflict for Christians, or at least it should not be. The cultural upbringing of Pentecostals encourages education as preparation for the life's work God has chosen for each individual. It is understood that the career chosen will always be within the context of Christ's purpose in one's life.

This is not a demeaning of individuality. Rather, the culture of the Pentecostal assumes that a devoted life to Christ and an internalizing of the Holy Scriptures yield the highest possible degree of personal happiness and success.

There is the predication that man is born to give glory to God. The more nearly one approximates the fulfillment of this goal, the greater his earthly reward and personal happiness.

Education is not an automatic and linear guarantee of success. If this were true, all highly educated individuals would be successful. And if success is to be associated in any measure with happiness, all highly educated people would be happy.

Success to the Pentecostal, and to every Christian, is to know the Lord Jesus Christ: This is at once the most intellectual and wisest decision of a man's life—to choose Jesus Christ as personal Lord. Having allied oneself to Jesus Christ, the Christian centers his life in this commitment. Religion is no longer an ancillary notion but a formal means of living out gratitude for having been brought into the family of God by Jesus Christ. This is success.

In the pursuit of living out this success, education becomes a natural act. One who loves God desires to know about God's world. With a heightened sense of God's presence in the world, he acquiring of knowledge is a progressive revelation of the glorious God in the personal life. It is not the creation of new knowledge, but the discovery of what God has created.

Because man is not developing or creating new knowledge, there is no logical way for one man to declare his superiority over others. Knowledge that is new to the individual was in the mind of God even before the Creation. In man's determination to learn, he only discovers the greatness of God. If all of this works as Pentecostals believe it should, the more a person learns, the greater his love for God the Creator.

From Outside. Non-Pentecostals, even Christians who do not believe in speaking with other tongues, have a tendency to target Pentecostals as being anti-intellectual. No debate is invited by the critics. There is just the categorical denigration of Pentecostals as being unlearned.

It is a subtle method, age-old, which avoids the issue of truth. Call a man "ignorant," and one excuses the responsibility for listening to what he has to say. In the philosophical form of social communication, ignorance is the approach which says, "You are wrong. You are stupid. Therefore, I do not have to listen to you."

Pentecostals have no argument for a monopoly on truth. The door is open. Pentecostals freely admit that except for the grace of God, there would be no current outpouring of the Holy Spirit. This is not a work of man but the work of God. It is not exclusive to those who have received. The Holy Spirit is available to all. Joel prophesied of these times that the Holy Spirit would be poured out "upon all flesh" (Joel 2:28).

Further, the Holy Spirit baptism is not to be cherished by a few who make it virtually impossible for others to receive the Holy Spirit. Every Christian is eligible to receive the Holy Spirit, thus qualifying to become a practicing Pentecostal.

Those who refuse the doctrine of Pentecost are sympathetically viewed by Pentecostals as having stopped short of discovering and receiving knowledge that indeed leads to ultimate intellectualism: communion and fellowship with the Creator This is not a presumption of higher IQ but an assertion that the wise man will follow Christ's bidding.

This must not be construed to imply that to speak in tongues is to be a learned man in worldly terms. What it does imply is that it is a prudent man who chooses Christ, and wise is the man who shares Christ with others (Proverbs 11:30).

If all this means that Pentecostals must live in the shadow of the halls of ivy, so be it. For this they will not be judged. But if there is failure to carry out the Great Commission of Jesus Christ, there will be judgment. Refusal to share the faith is tantamount to denying the faith. For this ignorance and rebellion, souls will perish.

By no means is the foregoing explanation intended to demean scholarly contributions by those who do not profess Christianity. Humanitarian accomplishments stand in their own merit. The greater point is that works, of themselves, do not justify man's entrance into heaven. Further, the works of man will eventually perish, while the soul of man will live eternally.

The kingdom of Christ upon earth is not to promote glorious works of man's hands, but to restore man to fellowship with his Creator. For the Pentecostal, it is Christ first and then education.

Those who are Christ's are compelled to avail themselves of every opportunity for improvement. To have a God-given opportunity to improve one's personal position and not to do so is to violate the will of God: "Therefore to him that knoweth to do good, and doeth it not, to him it is sin" (James 4:17).

Myth 6: If Elected to Public Office, Pentecostals Would Make Everyone Live According to Pentecostal Social Values

Before Pat Robertson even threw his hat into the ring, in the 1988 presidential campaign, Democratic National Committee chairman Paul G. Kirk, Jr., sent a letter to 50,000 people whom Democrats thought might consider countering a possible Robertson candidacy. According to the letter, Robertson "openly and aggressively advocates political action to achieve his primary goal—making America a place where everyone has the same extremist values and views of morality."

Kirk further warned that Robertson would like to "abolish public education, defeat the Equal Rights Amendment, outlaw abortion, require a quota of 'born-again Christians' in civil service jobs, and launch a massive military buildup."[5]

Robertson, accusing Kirk of "anti-Christian bigotry," demanded an apology. "Am I to understand the Democratic Party proposes to disenfranchise all Christians?" he asked.

DNC spokesman Terry Michael said there was no reason for Kirk to apologize. "The fund-raising letter did not address Pat Robertson's religious beliefs or the religious beliefs of any American," he said. "It addressed what we regard as the radical right-wing political agenda of Robertson."

Man's history is replete with love-hate stories of the law. It is much like the dictum "Can't live with it, and can't live without it."

When man does not like what the law requires, he sees law as an abomination. But when man's desires are not readily attainable, or his fears containable, via the existing social structure, he has been known to declare: "There ought to be a law" with the conviction that whatever god or gods there be, such divines ought to be dutifully about the business of legalizing.

---

[5] Fund-raising letter sent by Paul Kirk, Jr., chairman of the Democratic National Committee in the fall of 1985.

Recorded history weaves its chronicle with religion consistently at the core of legal systems. There is a certain intertwining of religious laws with the whole of man's existence and developing social order. Even societies that have not been predicated in a certain religious system have found it necessary to incorporate religion as a component of the social system.

The charge we examine here is that Pentecostals are too legalistic. Assuming this proposition has legitimacy presumes a certain regimentation of thought that disallows man freedoms divinely given to man, or believed to be natural. This is a central issue to those who oppose Pentecostals' involvement in public affairs or public offices. Legalism in its extreme form predicates fundamentalism, or perhaps it is fundamentalism which begets legalism. Whichever, tolerance for alternative beliefs and behavior is limited, and the potential for aggression is maximized—or so goes the argument.

Fundamentalism in its extreme form predicates violence. In its ultimate form, fundamentalism may even dictate violence against nonmembers as, for example, in the case of the Shiite Muslims.

There have been insinuations that if Pentecostals should come into power, they would be equal in violence to Hitler and other such tyrants of history. Such critics insist that Pentecostals polarize issues and refuse dignity to those who are outside their theological borders. This polarization implemented into public law would deny all those not Pentecostal the right of free expression, or possibly forcibly deprive them of life and liberty.

Those who so harshly speculate on the mental and spiritual capabilities of Pentecostals to be public rulers miserably fail to know or comprehend the mind-set of Pentecostals. By nature, the Pentecostal is pressed with the issue of personal morality. Generally holding to the belief that one can fall from grace, sin, and be damned, believers do not have as a primary goal the correcting of the ills of society by crowd control. Grace is an individual matter; it cannot by definition be mandated by law.

The teachings of Jesus dealt generously with paying taxes, being obedient to the authorities, being a good neighbor, and practicing good business management. However, not once did He speak against the oppressive government of Rome or suggest to His followers that they should take up arms. "My kingdom is not of this world" (John 18:36) was His answer to those who wanted to take control of the government to usher in the kingdom of Christ.

Adam, in his fleshly and carnal appetite, became prodigal and departed from the ways of God. There is the earnest persuasion that hope for man and for society rests in God's divine intervention to save man from himself.

There is no hint of a militancy that would warrant arms and guns. The talk and language of those meetings and revivals that fanned like wildfire from east to west and west to east around 1900 was not of revolutions and wars, but of the power of God and eternal glory of Christ's church. Preachers did not thunder from pulpits of the damnation and devilment of politicians and government so much as they thundered confession and repentance of the individual.

The Pentecostal worldview is one of redemption for society via the individual. It does not necessarily emphasize wholesale societal repentance, though such is deemed possible. The worldview of the Pentecostal leans to a negative or gloomy perspective of man's ability to legislate or negotiate, via human government, universal harmony. Hope for mankind's survival depends upon choosing Christ as Savior. Thus, man's motives and desires come into alignment with divine ethics and the purity of God.

It should also be observed that all speculation of society's doom at the hands of Pentecostals in governmental leadership positions is without any historical precedent. There simply is no evidence that "tongues-speaking people" have ever sought to enslave or annihilate those not part of their faith.

To the contrary, there is enormous evidence that Pentecostals themselves have been unfairly accused and harshly treated in history. Pentecostals have been among the most repressed groups in communist countries. Countries dominated by Roman Catholicism have consistently enforced laws and policies making it difficult to impossible for Pentecostals to practice their faith in groups. It was not until 1981 that a religious freedom act was established in Spain. In much of the recent history of the Dominican Republic, a Roman Catholic archbishop has been a high government official dogmatically oppressing Evangelicals, including Pentecostals.

Pat Robertson is one of the most widely known tongues-speakers. It is particularly noteworthy that he has not to this date attempted to rally his political fort with a call to all those who "speak in tongues." Interestingly, Robertson has held credentials with the Southern Baptists, a quasi-conservative denomination that by its theology is not very warm on the practice of 'tongues." While Southern Baptists acknowledge the reality and practicality of tongues in the New Testament, the organizaional position is that the phenomenon served its purpose in New Testament times and has been relegated to the archives.

The major point of referring to Pat Robertson's political ventures is to establish that as a presidential candidate he did not ally his forces around religious banners. Potential candidates wisely enlist their supporters; however, this is not of itself an act of impropriety.

In truth, Robertson and all those who are politically akin to Robertson are tongues-speakers more closely allied with the advent of Charismatics. While there is no animosity between the Charismatic tongues-speakers and Pentecostals, they have sufficient theological and pragmatic variations to keep them in different channels. The common ground is the baptism of the Holy Spirit with tongues. Beyond this, diversity is extensive.

While Robertson has maintained friendly ties with the Pentecostals, he has continued his ministry in an arena that clearly has not been overflowing with classical Pentecostals. There is a reason for this pattern of behavior.

Robertson is identified with the Charismatic tongues-speakers, a segment generally comprised of members of mainstream churches. Intriguingly, the Charismatics' theology encourages hands-on responsibility for bringing human government into form for the return of Jesus to set up His kingdom on earth. Yet, while active political involvement may be encouraged by Charismatics, the second commandment of "Love thy neighbour as thyself" is respected. Christian charity prevents even Charismatics from the reckless abandon of treating opponents, unbelievers, or sinners with the ruthlessness of which tongues-speakers are accused.

Tongues-speakers have no interest in taking the law into their own hands. It constitutes rebellion and anarchy. The Pentecostal's primary concentration is to walk in harmony with Jesus Christ, thus living a just and holy life of service to God and man. The use of governmental force to establish a moral society is illegitimate by nature. Gaining public office by proper procedure is allowable, but holding public office is a subfunction of the believer's life and not the primary purpose for existence. Certainly, the ambitious militancy of fanatical fundamentalists is forbidden.

There is an irony involved in this issue of legalism. Integral to the faith is a belief that Jesus Christ will return to earth to reign as king for 1,000 years. During that 1,000 years no outward sin will be manifested, and Satan will not be present to tempt anyone to sin.

It is perhaps the very belief in this "ruling with the rod of iron" that allows Pentecostals to be patient within the present context of government. In essence, Jesus himself will correct the errors of human injustice and establish a universal system of government providing equity for every man. Man's best work then is to prepare his heart for the return of Jesus.

Pentecostals incorporate into their policies the right of

individuals to refuse to bear arms, or to choose noncombat alternatives in the event of war. Denominational support is assured to individuals who make these decisions. At the same time, those who bear arms suffer no sanctions.

What is not condoned is lack of patriotism, unless the government is opposed to the truths of the Bible. In such an event, Pentecostals are in the difficult position of not cooperating with evil but not bearing violence against their native country. One can be a good citizen and not be Pentecostal; but if one is Pentecostal, being a good citizen is presupposed.

Estimates in the early 1980s projected that as many as 200,000 Soviet Pentecostal men would not bear Soviet arms. However, there is not a shred of evidence that these men attempted any act of violence to overthrow the Soviet system, despite the violence done to the men by the Soviets. Even superficial research of Pentecostals will soon lay to rest the argument of legalism in terms of public affairs or government.

In effect, it may be true that Pentecostals and many other Protestants place greater emphasis on social restrictions. However, it is significant to separate desired behavior from the force of the law. To optimize is not to mandate. There is a quantum difference between discussion of social rules that pertain to victorious Christian living and the use of force in the name of God. There are no papal armies in Pentecostal history.

The problem of legalism among Pentecostals is more an internal application than an external judgment of non-Pentecostals. It is more social than doctrinal. It is an act of self-discipline to attain a holy life, not a social strategy to place others in bondage. Those who are concerned about societal order may rest their fears of Pentecostals' using force in political leadership.

Let it be repeated that history records the use of force in the name of God by most religions. However, when these religions are ranked by their willingness to use force to accomplish holy purposes, Pentecostals will place with the peacemakers.

CHAPTER 5

Controversy Surrounding Pentecostals

▼ ▼ ▼ ▼ ▼ ▼ ▼ ▼ ▼ ▼ ▼ ▼

Why opponents persecute Pentecostals largely depends on who is "throwing the stone." What is certain is that prejudice exists. Therefore, sociological principles for analysis are useful as would be true of prejudice in any other form.

Criticizing or persecuting others is often a consequence of feeling threatened. Threat is related to the fear of loss of power, loss of self-esteem, loss of material possessions, or the concern that human beings of lesser social worth are socially infringing on personal territory.

Fear and hatred are most likely to result in action when the threat is from those on the social ladder only one rung away—either just above or just below. Most of the criticism of Pentecostals has come from those higher on the social ladder. Established mainstream churches have felt the loss as many of their members have switched their allegiance and finances to the Pentecostal Movement.

Criticism of Pentecostals by the lower socioeconomic classes has been diffused, which may be attributable to their lack of organizational skills. Less fortunate peoples have fewer communication skills and fewer techniques for using the skills they have. Frustrations tend to be verbal or physical, personally exercised, and delivered over a brief period of time. Most of this form of opposition occurred in the earlier days of Pentecostalism when the preaching and teaching openly labeled as "sin" certain habits and actions common to the lower socioeconomic classes and yet allowable in mainstream churches.

As churches were built and ministers trained, services held

in the open air, tents, and public halls became less frequent and popular. Since those who wanted to attend a Pentecostal church did so voluntarily, whatever was said or done was primarily to a closed audience. Violent or verbal attacks began to decrease.

On the other hand, as Pentecostal denominations were birthed and grew into viable organizations, denominations that had initially ignored the tongues-speakers became concerned. Conferences and study commissions were called to explain the phenomenon of speaking in other tongues. Vatican II by the Roman Catholics validated tongues. The Commission on Doctrine in 1969 applauded the emphasis on the Bible but cautioned Catholic tongues-speakers to stay in the fold of the mother church. Tozer, a leader of the Protestant Christian and Missionary Alliance Church, which at first was receptive to the Pentecostal Movement but then cooled its interest, summed up the position of many of those outside the Pentecostal Movement when he said, "Seek not. Forbid not."

Following are plausible reasons for the historical and continuing opposition against Pentecostals:

1. *Speaking in other tongues implies that the speaker has a direct connection with God.* It is only a 25-cent local call. Or the fax machine just zips it right to heaven and back—in seconds. For those outside, this is tantamount to special privileges. It is unfair access or denial of equality, both terribly offensive. "Who do they think they are?" is the natural comeback that fosters battlegrounds.

2. *Speaking in other tongues implies a greater piety than that of those who do not speak in tongues.* Persons on this frequency are able to receive information, insights, and instruction not available to other Christians or non-Christians. Those outside this "higher spiritual life" are demeaned in their rank and authority. Communion with God on an intimate level tends to pyramid authority, with God at the top. Thus, traditional rank order is challenged. Secular and sacred governments skeptical of Pentecostals also suspect their submissiveness.

3. *Speaking in other tongues implies that there is only one way to receive certain heavenly blessings.* While there is no declared war, the message is that other paths to God either are not utilitarian, not practical, or are dead wrong. Ultimate elitism is inherent. Pluralism is dethroned. Ecumenism is dead. Bumper stickers such as "My God's alive—sorry about yours," while not peculiarized by Pentecostals, nevertheless suggest the power of divisiveness that results from religious elitism.

Groups That May Take Issue With Pentecostal Doctrine

Mainline Churches. Speaking in other tongues is a phenomenon that has drawn significant interest and numbers from mainstream churches. The loss of finances and parishioners has been ample reason for alarm among church fathers.

At a time when mainstream churches were bogged down in social and political action, the wave of speaking in tongues called attention back to spiritual things. The consequence was that traditional loyalties were broken. Tongues-speakers tended to give to the ministries where they felt the Spirit was moving. Tight budgets of mainstream churches entered a new era of crisis.

Tongues-speakers are the new kids. New arrivals are supposed to know their place, be welcomed by the old, and yield to the customs of the neighborhood.

Concern about a social movement, even if it is a religious one, is minimal until it trespasses "private property." Tongues-speakers moved uptown and bought property on Main Street. They did not ask permission. They did not yield to the traditions. Principles, ideas, and objects of merit are likely to be resented if the right to belong is presumed, rather than requested.

Tongues-speakers brought action to the pulpit and pew and reemphasized the altar as a place of God's meeting man. If there were excesses, the excesses did not displace the honest results of revivals, prayer meetings, and spiritual emphases.

Added to all this, the worship services of the tongues-speakers used a variety of instruments. Laypeople were allowed to be involved in worship, and upbeat music was an attraction for the worshipers.

Mainstream churches found themselves in a difficult and embarrassing situation. To declare the tongues movement a work of the devil required biblical reasons, and there would be the danger of losing large numbers of parishioners. A lack of growth, even decline, had created a vacuum. Added to all this, the baby boomers were discovering that yuppie life has no panacea in a materialistic world. Revival and reformation were a must to meet the challenge of the Holy Spirit movement.

Roman Catholics. Tongues is a heavenly language that can be obtained via prayer. It cannot be bought, sold, or learned in a secular setting. Tongues is a prayer language that elevates the believer to priesthood. The individual can enter into the very presence of God without the assistance or permission of any other human.

Sore spot: This makes every believer a priest. Immediately, Roman Catholic and sister churches are threatened. A rationale must be offered justifying why tongues-speakers are out of order if they refuse to acknowledge or be submissive to higher church authority. Study commissions and rulings of mainstream churches have focused on this problem. Obviously, the ultimate objective is to ensure that mainstream tongues-speakers do not "bolt from the flock."

Donald Gelpi is a noted Roman Catholic author and theologian. In his book *Pentecostalism*, he proposes a theological approach to maintaining the Roman Catholic Church as the legitimate body to administer the charismatic blessing of tongues. He notes that the tongues experience is not a new one. There are two theologies offered to explain the experience of the Holy Spirit. For the tongues-speakers of mainstream churches, often referred to as Charismatics, tongues is seen as a Paschal event related to the slaying of the lamb in Egypt. The significance of this approach is that it represents the Holy Spirit as emphasizing the Lamb of God who died for our sins.

The second approach is from the Book of Luke, called the

"Lucan" account. The Holy Spirit came on the Day of Pentecost, 40 days after the Passover. The Jewish feast of Pentecost symbolized the alliance between God and Israel at Mount Sinai. This covenant included the Ten Commandments and affirmed God's plan for abiding with His chosen people and blessing them. In similar fashion, current Pentecostals accept the Lucan and Acts accounts to represent Jesus' *new* covenant with believers.

Gelpi, having made this distinction of origins, proceeds to affirm that not every believer is given tongues. However, those who do receive the gift then must exercise it within the eucharistic community, that is, the Roman Catholic Church.

That contemporary Pentecostalism occurred in many parts of the world simultaneously presents a flaw in Gelpi's philosophy. Further, many of the early Pentecostals did not receive the Holy Spirit baptism with tongues while worshiping within the context of a mainstream church. Theology must be placed within the context of the history of Jesus' church, not man-made organizations.

What Gelpi provides is a structure whereby all those who speak in tongues are Christian. But the picture is of two streams flowing in the same direction: one straight and with clear waters (Charismatic, in the Roman Catholic tradition) and the other with curves and dips and the water not so clear (Pentecostal). He does not overtly disqualify Pentecostals, but he does not place them in a legitimate context of practicing the charismatic gifts of the Holy Spirit.

Theology aside, there is a practical aspect of these two perspectives. The theological orientations dictate different organizational structures. Thus, there is little probability of convergence into a singular organizational structure, nor is there hope for ecumenism.

The Intellectual Community. With all the fury of throwing the tomahawk to the ground to declare war, promoting the idea of a heavenly language divides the haves and the have-nots. One of the highest premiums placed on interdisciplinary studies is the mastery of more than one language.

tongues-speakers, including those who are poorly educated illiterate, believe that a foreign language can be obtained instantly. This gift is not accompanied by a grammar book with dictionary and verb tense.

To the academic man without faith, this idea is an insult not worthy of discussion. It gets discarded as garbage, and those who would believe such preposterous notions are pitied, despised, or shunned.

The antagonist insists

1. There is no scientific proof of heaven.
2. There is no scientific proof of a perfect language.
3. No person could possibly be enabled to speak in a foreign language simply because of prayer.

Regardless of the nature of a possession, if the owner of the possession is perceived to be of lesser mental abilities than "normal" folks, those not possessing it feel no envy. There is no middle ground. The rationalism of scientific analysis is an impasse, probably forever destined to separate Pentecostals from those who abhor the doctrine and practice of tongues.

Further Opposition. Tongues is a pure and heavenly language, without flaw, profanity, or error. The Tower of Babel was a work of the devil, for which man suffered loss of the perfect language of our father Adam. Tongues is a reestablishing of heavenly communication between God and man. As part of Christ's ministry on earth, He authorized the coming of the Holy Spirit, which Pentecostals believe included tongues.

Opponents scoff at the idea of a heavenly language. They insist that the tongues experience is not a heavenly manifestation. Antagonists perceive tongues to range from "ecstatic utterances" of self-induced frenzies to demonic chanting.

Opponents' Response Choices

The criticisms and critics of Pentecostals are numerous and varied. The intensity of their opposition also varies. There are those who don't like, those who hate, those who ignore, and those who openly resist. Ultimately, five options are available for expression of prejudice against any person, object, or idea:

1. *Ignore the phenomenon.* Dismiss it as being less than worthy of attention. Don't talk about it. Don't write about it. Don't fuel opposition. Don't think about it. Treat it as being nonexistent.

2. *Criticize the phenomenon.* Two approaches are available for criticism:

   a. *Soft approach:* "Much ado about nothing." Refute by demeaning. "This too shall pass." "Not important."

   b. *Hard approach:* Attempt to denigrate without getting personally involved. Say it is evil, communistic, insane, or of the devil. If words can dethrone, it is cheaper than action, and less threatening to the person exercising prejudice.

3. *Take specific action.* Oppose by peaceful means or violent procedures. Sanctions exercised may range from rebuke to persecution, from denial of freedom to loss of life.

4. *Create an alternative.* In an attempt to detract from the object of the antagonism, develop or create and implement an alternative. The challenge to present an alternative is awesome. Stealing thunder is not an easy task. Convincing people to turn aside from a burning bush is a formidable assignment. Man tends to devote energies to the issue that raises his adrenalin.

5. *Join the enemy.* Collapse the categories. Bring home the army. Get out the truce flag. "If you can't lick 'em, join 'em." Try to accomplish the very best possible compromise. However, the one who brings out the flag is likely to put the most in "to sweeten the pot."

The Pentecostals' Response

How victims respond to prejudice is conditional. In certain forms, opposition can encourage victims to band together and share commonly in fulfilling the mission and accomplishing the goal of the group. On the positive side, it serves to clarify, purify, and sort out weaknesses. Or prejudice may be destructive, creating pain, confusion, disorientation, and discouragement among victims. Finally, there is prejudice that simply is ignored by the intended victims, because the effects of the prejudice are too abstract or remote.

Recent years have brought about some tragedies in prominent Pentecostal/Charismatic ministries, for example, Jim Bakker, Jimmy Swaggart. These tragedies have been political fodder for feeding the prejudice machine against Pentecostals. The deluge of news coverage has fostered not-so-subtle implications that Pentecostal organizations do a poor job of housekeeping. Whether this negativism has been intentional or malicious is not the issue of this writing.

In the face of embarrassing publicity and stinging prejudice, the Pentecostal ranks have continued rapid growth. Opponents fail to recognize that the camp of tongues-speakers is extremely diverse. Cannonballs shot at particular ministries may devastate a person, business, or church, but the tremor effect does not succeed in deterring the larger movement.

While a sense of loss may be present following these events, the phenomenon of tongues-speaking is not one of stardom or personality cults. Leaders are esteemed, but the Pentecostal experience is not given by leaders. Therefore, the validity of the experience is not to be questioned when leadership fails. There are no gurus. There are no high priests. There are no popes. Leaders wisely refer to themselves as servants. If they fail morally or spiritually, it is not God's failure but man's failure.

In addition, there is sufficient diversity among tongues-speakers to keep most of them from feeling any personal liability for any specific failure of leaders. The failure of man is in no way an indictment of God.

Pentecostals do not think of themselves as being a part of a social movement, but rather of a spiritual force. The concept of a movement is macro thinking, global in concept. Speaking in other tongues is a private experience. It often occurs while alone or in small groups, which fact makes it difficult to relate the experience to all the tongues-speakers in the world, except on a theological basis.

Reactions to Prejudice

Reactions to and options chosen by Pentecostals to counter prejudice have taken several forms:

1. *Adjust and correct.* Valid criticisms have been received and action taken. For example, to clear the air on snake-handling, an international Pentecostal church's top leader repudiated the practice in 1915.

2. *Ignore the criticism.* To ignore is always a choice. Prejudice that is difficult to address is perhaps better left unanswered.

3. *Teach and preach.* Primarily directed to believers, this approach perhaps is most effective in minimizing internal damage. It also serves to prepare the listeners for more appropriate responses to future acts of prejudice.

4. *Write.* Writings fall into two categories: (a) those for internal consumption and (b) those for external consumption. The first tend to be of a friendly, informative, and constructive nature, while the second tend to be critical in analysis, defensive in nature, and with an appeal for understanding.

5. *Initiate legal action.* In a few situations legal action has been threatened or taken in order to counter prejudice. An example of this approach is illustrated by the Church of God's establishing a policy defining the use of the epithet "Holy Roller" as libel.[1]

6. *Pray.* To pray for the enemy is a basic part of the Christian faith practiced by Pentecostals. This is taught as the

---

[1]Conn, p. 131.

most effective means.

7. *Take political action.* Writing letters, running for political office, lobbying, and so forth, are all legal and valid options in the American society. However, there is the consistent caution that believers must not do this for their own personal gain or fame.

8. *Integrate.* Fostering and establishing friendship and business ties with the critics is acceptable so long as it does not lead to compromise. Joining interdenominational ministerial organizations, becoming a member of the Chamber of Commerce, and getting involved in charitable organizations are popular methods for achieving status and silencing critics.

9. *Professionalize.* Obtaining a professional degree from a secular state or private institution is an established pattern for gaining social acceptance and disarming critics. It is difficult to criticize a schoolteacher, counselor, or administrator. People with these degrees and careers have paid the same dues as the person who is criticizing. Religious affiliation may become a secondary issue in a professional setting.

10. *Move uptown.* Nice property and a beautiful building in a respectable location tend to decrease opposition. It is the old "co-opt" principle, and it also works with religion.

11. *Educate.* Build or buy schools, colleges, and universities. This is a tried-and-true method of upward social mobility.

12. *Train the clergy.* Acceptance by mainstream churches will not be granted until the clergy of a new movement are trained on a comparable level. Currently, every major international Pentecostal organization places strong emphasis on the education of ministers.

13. *Publicize.* Purchase time on TV and radio or space in newspapers, magazines, and high school yearbooks. Establish public relations departments. Participate in county fairs and community charities. These techniques make possible reaching large numbers of people quickly with a positive message of goodwill.

Summary remarks are important to the conclusion of our dealing with stones thrown at Pentecostals. Jesus said that He had been persecuted and His believers would also be persecuted. Being persecuted for Christ's sake is considered a high and noble privilege. Josephus, a secular historian of Jesus' times, wrote of the opposition to Christ and His followers and how such opposition fueled increased loyalty to the cause.

This nonviolent approach tends to greatly frustrate opponents. Even in communist countries, the government questions how to deal with the peaceful but uncompromising Pentecostals. Pray for your enemy (Luke 6:28); if he strikes you on one cheek, turn the other (Matthew 5:39); and go the extra mile (Matthew 5:41) are unusual dictums for countering enemy moves.

What matters to Pentecostals is that the method works. Their peaceful attitude toward opposition has prevented the waste of energies. And their mission is not social acceptance but Christlike living and the sharing of their faith.

CHAPTER 6

From a Look Back to the Road Ahead

▼ ▼ ▼ ▼ ▼ ▼ ▼ ▼ ▼ ▼ ▼

Social movements that survive tend to institutionalize. Numbers of Pentecostals have moved to denominational status. Thousands of independent local churches and fellowship bodies have tongues-speaking as a focal point of their orientation. Yet, incredibly, there remains the momentum of a social movement among these vast, but amorphous, ranks. The message communicated portrays a sense of urgency: God is sending revival— revival that includes baptizing believers with the Holy Spirit.

What is ahead for the Pentecostal Movement? Will its future be one of continued expansion? Will the revival continue? Will the various factions move toward any confluence of theology and organization? The ability to see the road ahead is enhanced by a look at the road already traveled.

The contemporary revival of Pentecostalism happened at a fortuitous time in the development of technology. Electricity, telephones, radios, televisions, automobiles, airplanes, typewriters, copiers, computers, fax machines, subways, superhighways, and express passenger trains are all part of the modern world.

Commensurate with unprecedented scientific development, the 20th century also has experienced numerous major wars and natural disasters. World population growth has doubled three times in less than a hundred years, thus increasing the number of suffering people, or those at risk.

Man has yearned to believe, to find meaning in life, and to hope for a peaceful world. The League of Nations and the United Nations respectively were organized after the two great wars in a bold international move to prevent man from destroying himself. Earthquakes, tornadoes, typhoons, floods, fires, disease, famine, human error, terrorism, technological disasters, revolution, debt-ridden governments, and communism shake our world, leaving hearts fearful, yet seemingly with few places to retreat or find refuge.

National and international statesmen are in premium demand. The news media makes it difficult for one to have a halo. Our best men are flawed when TV cameras have stopped rolling and the presses have been turned off. Who will lead us out of the morass? Who will dare to presume that he has the answer for our troubled world? Is there hope? Is peace possible?

Precisely when man is the most disillusioned and discouraged, he is fertile soil for acceptance of previously unknown or rejected ideas. A way out of the dilemma is welcomed, even if it calls for sacrifice. Which way to go depends on which doors open. The latitude runs full range—including war, social causes, suicide, drugs, and religion. No options for exit are nixed if pain will be diminished or it is believed that life will be better or different on the other side of the door of opportunity.

The Pentecostal explosion is now universal, including hundreds of millions of adherents in Third World and oppressed countries. Organization in these countries has been very difficult. Religions not approved by the governmental system are often disenfranchised, limiting or forbidding rights to own property, hold meetings, and travel. Efforts to move toward denominational status and institutionalization have been and will be difficult, frustrating, and plagued with political and ecclesiastical red tape. Many of the historic challenges and obstacles of Pentecostalism in America will be repeated as tongues-speakers in oppressed countries seek to survive and organize. In a sense, the wheel must be reinvented.

Religious people not part of the mainstream and who have not been cooperative with governments are often denied jobs, education, and ownership. The result is a maintaining or lowering of one's social status, and perhaps standard of living. In countries that open doors to new freedoms, the disinherited have little with which to parlay or bargain entrance into the social mainstream. Freedom without negotiability is a mixed blessing.

Pentecostals often are among the oppressed in Third World countries and have vivid memories of persecution, while they have watched other religious groups be favored. As freedoms are extended, religious believers who have been persecuted will not look to the nominal or co-opted churches for assistance and guidance. In some cases the state-approved churches were in open or silent assent to the persecution of minority religious groups, including Pentecostals. The result is that churches which were cooperative with oppressive governments are often perceived as being a part of the Antichrist's system. Distrust is not healed via a government document with vague language of "new freedoms."

It is hypothesized that Pentecostals in oppressed countries will look to those with whom they are closest of kin. Independent churches can offer only limited assistance. Nominal churches with Charismatic groups are limited by bureaucracy that reduces their Charismatic community to a subculture. The logical answer is that these tongues-speakers in remote parts of the world will look to the traditional or classical Pentecostals for consultation, discourse, and fellowship.

A burden of proof will fall upon Pentecostal organizations outside oppressed and emerging countries. Compromise in any form that would indicate co-optation by nominal churches or secular society will send a negative signal to tongues-speakers in oppressed countries who are looking for guidance and affiliation. Pentecostal organizations perceived as compromising with liberal churches will be rejected by Third World Pentecostals. Christians who lately suffered religious persecution will not be open to affiliation or association with churches or denominations that were cooperative with oppressive governments.

What is certain is that the tongues movement has become a fixture, a staple in the world of religion. The Holy Spirit movement, or at least the controversy, has made inroads into most camps of Christendom. The diversity will continue. The theological distance between different camps will probably increase.

New words and definitions will search to explore brotherhood, or explain and justify separatism. There may even be a growing tendency to feud. However, the phenomenon is larger than any group, congregation, or denomination. Pentecostalism is here to stay.

CHAPTER 7

The Pilgrimage: A Perspective

▼ ▼ ▼ ▼ ▼ ▼ ▼ ▼ ▼ ▼ ▼ ▼

My dad missed World War II because of a previous ankle injury, but he and Mom faithfully sought to serve our country as honest, productive citizens. Those duties also included certain ministerial responsibilities.

Our lives were lived in a world of strong religious commitment that was inclusive of our past, our present, and our future. It made sense to us, and in it we found fulfillment. We believed that when a person meets Christ, he experiences the beginning of eternal life. We termed this introduction to Christ being "born again."

The term "born again" was not a mystical term abstracted from philosophy. Even children of our culture understood that "born again" was a real-life experience describing the impact of a person's acceptance of Jesus Christ as one's Savior and Lord. Subsequent to the experience, it was expected that the new convert would readily settle down to honest work (if he had not already done so), arrange to pay any bad debts, quit drinking alcohol and using tobacco, become regularly involved in a local church, develop a spiritual responsibility to his family and community, and in general form a testimony that would assure acquaintances that his old master, Satan, was no longer in charge.

During the late '50s, there was a national renewal and people of many denominations became excited about this "born-again" experience. We were a little puzzled about all the commotion, as though a new Bible had just been discovered. It seemed to us that the truths of God's Word were rather obvious. How could "born again" be new, when Jesus had told Nicodemus it was the only way to heaven? (John 3:3).

If we were puzzled at the first, there was more to come. A new wave made "healing" the attraction of the religious masses. Folks seemed delighted to discover that the Lord was still able to do what He did in the New Testament. As for our home and church, prayer for God to heal had been as normal as eating ever since we had started to breathe. Besides, healing was a hallmark of the New Testament Christians.

There was a measurable degree of excitement and apprehension as we heard of and read about people of many nominal denominations who were "born again" and "healed." Church fathers were optimistic that these new converts would soon join with us in a devoted and "old-fashioned" walk with the Lord.

About the time we were laying carpet in the church and padding the pews, we were chagrined to discover that our new brothers in the Lord were determined to stay in their native churches and be "instruments of revival."

"Surely," they told us, "the Lord will be pleased with our dedication to revitalize spiritually dead churches." They would continue to attend church with their families who had not yet "seen the light." We puzzled that they took their new treasures back to the cathedrals they described as, and we believed to be, full of spiritual bones.

Comfort was found in the quiet knowledge that many of these new believers did not understand the Rapture—the second advent of the Lord. If they but understood the promise of Jesus to come back to earth, surely they would find themselves in the harvest fields with believers of kindred spirit.

Our comfort was short-lived. The Six-Day War in Israel in the late '60s precipitated many new articles and books on the Second Coming. Before long, there were so many theories of the Second Coming that confusion prompted discouragement. Sadly, the hope for Christ's return was whittled away. Some said Jesus would not come back until the world is perfected by man. Others said that He would come back, but it would be at an indefinite time in the future, thus irrelevant to our times. Still others insisted His return would be in the middle or latter part of the Great Tribulation.

Great Tribulation! How did they find out about this time when God will vent His anger on a sinful world? How dared they insist that Christians will be left here to be a part of the kingdom of the Antichrist, who will be the worldly lord of the Great Tribulation until he is dethroned by Jesus? Theological jargon bombarded us until the simplicity of our faith and lives was shaken. The faith that had been precious and beautiful was beginning to have tattered edges, spots, and blemishes.

Before we had grasped the theories, philosophies, and theologies of our new brothers in Christ, the whole issue of the return of Christ was softened and put on a back burner. So many wise Christian heads were disagreeing about when Christ would return that the issue was tabled for discussion at a future time. Christians have too much to do to spend all their time talking. A sense of urgency demands action, not just discussion.

No time was to be lost. Quietly a decision was made by our leaders. If the new brothers in Christ would not come and join with us, we would go uptown and build nice churches like theirs. If they could go to heaven with the "full blessing" in air-conditioned cathedrals, so could we.

This decision never reached a vote or open forum. It just happened. And it happened so naturally, so easily. We sent our sons and daughters off to college to advance their training for the ministry. At home our faithfulness to God yielded bountiful fruit as righteous living and hard work raised our standard of living. It is divinely ordained that holy living increases net worth, since frivolity and waste are eliminated from economics. Joy is from within and is not measured by material possessions.

We could no longer argue for our identity on the grounds of a "born-again" experience. Our quiet faith in the healing power of Jesus had been disrupted by crusaders with "unique" anointing to pray for the sick for divine healing. Our hope of the return of Jesus to make sense out of the nonsense had been shattered by "educated" new brothers in Christ. They insisted that the nature and time of the Second Coming could not be defined; therefore, in the interest of Christian unity, it should not be a focus of discussion.

All the while we were finding that God was not any bigger in magnificent edifices than in modest buildings. Sobered by our discovery that what impresses man does not necessarily impress God, we determined to renew ourselves in walking with the Holy Spirit. Running like a golden thread through our heritage, we knew that sincere, fervent prayer will always touch the heart of God and authorize and activate the Holy Spirit to work in our personal lives.

"Not by might, nor by power, but by my spirit" (Zechariah 4:6) had been our motto. We revived it, and we were revived. A new courage took hold. We would rejoice in the power of the Holy Spirit, a fact that had peculiarized us among all the "born-again" believers. Even those who called themselves Christians but refused the stigma of "born again" tended to view "Holy Spirit Christians" as a distinctive group.

The Holy Spirit revitalized our ranks, and our courage was renewed. A new surge of brotherhood and evangelism evolved with missionary proportions. Where confusion and discouragement had weakened our resolve, a fresh burst of devotion and zeal heralded old landmarks and established new horizons.

For so long we had thought that God could bless only those of a particular cultural and doctrinal persuasion. Now we knew there were "sheep of another fold" that were also children of God. We had learned with great difficulty that they did not have to be like us, and that we could not be like them in their lifestyles. We reaffirmed: God rewards those that walk by faith, in grace, and by love.

This was a valuable lesson, and it was just in time. Knocking at our door was a stranger to tell us that the world had discovered our best-kept secret: the work of the Holy Spirit.

We had not meant to keep it a secret. In fact, we had tried to give it away. However, we had been rebuffed until discouragement persuaded us to retreat. When we had told folks that we spoke in tongues, interpreted, and prophesied, they had automatically assumed that we also handled snakes and did other strange things. We had honorably resorted to a quiet faith without fanfare. The glare of the spotlight had blinded us and we sought to find a role backstage.

Coming to the front lines in the second wave were fresh recruits who claimed to have from 10 to 25 more Holy Spirit gifts than we had ever heard of or witnessed. Added to this was their ability to get a five-second answer from God on whether to have lunch at Shoney's or McDonald's and whether to drink Pepsi or Coke with their lunch. We listened as they prayed for God to use them for miracles of healing and deliverance, yet they needed an answer from heaven to know where to be in church on Sunday.

Our inner sanctum was violated. We were demeaned. We had told the world for 100 years that the Holy Spirit would abide only in a clean temple, holy and sanctified. This second wave said they could participate in social activities or habits we had called "sin," and they could still speak in tongues. It was a devastating blow. Our halo was cracked. Our testimony was at risk. Our existence was threatened.

Where could we go? Our shoreline had been eroded. Had we been so wrong to believe in a separate life of holiness unto the Lord? Had we incurred opposition because of our expectation that Christians ought to walk in holiness and righteousness all the days of our lives? (Luke 1:75). Had we been too narrow for our own good? Was it possible that we had created our own obstacles in living out our faith?

David found a place of direction in times of question. He went to the house of God (see Psalm 73, especially v. 17). One of the great virtues of a walk in the Holy Spirit is the importance placed on gathering together in worship. David went to church and got his priorities in order. His heart received peace and his spirit was renewed. Likewise, our steadiness yielded fruit. We had not ceased to be faithful to God's house; this fact stabilized us in time of storm.

If the years have unfolded certain lessons to us, they are simple lessons:

We have learned . . .
>that "the word of the Lord endureth for ever" (1 Peter 1:25) and that "the just shall live by faith" (Galatians 3:11).

We have learned . . .
>that steadiness and consistency are more valuable than fanfare. Not all that glitters is gold.

We have learned . . .
>that we must walk in the light of the gospel without measuring our progress in comparison to others. To violate our godly conscience is to sin, regardless of how it is defined by man.

We have learned . . .
>that walking in the Spirit prohibits us from using our liberty as a cloak for maliciousness (1 Peter 2:16).

We have learned . . .
>that it is better to have the approval of God than the applause of man.

We have learned . . .
>that the loudness of the rejoicing is not related to the strength of the commitment.

We have learned . . .
>that those who walk in the Spirit do not glory in their gifts, but in the Giver. We rejoice for the pleasure to serve and bring honor to the Giver, Jesus Christ.

In our solitude, we rediscovered prayer. In prayer, we found strength to go on. The issues became less confusing. The goal became clear, and the course a matter of resolution. Prayer refreshed us and became our anchor against the storm and our motivator to fulfill our mission.

All our tribulations have but the more deeply anchored our faith. We are the more convinced that Christ is soon coming for His church, made up of all those who have claimed Jesus as Lord of their lives. Urgency drives us to reach our world with the message of Christ, and the Holy Spirit is empowering us to go.

Our ship has been steadied. Our course is determined. We know not what course others will take, but as for us, "to live is Christ, and to die is gain" (Philippians 1:21). We will hold to the straight path without frills and lace. Perhaps we shall deny ourselves some liberties that others maintain are acceptable. The denial is no sacrifice. We prefer not to be a stumbling block, but an encourager.

The sifting is the work of Christ. We have the perfect confidence that He does all things well. As for us, we shall continue to walk as we have been walking, enjoying the benefits of Pentecost.